Twayne's United States Authors Series

EDITOR OF THIS VOLUME

Lewis Leary

University of North Carolina

Thomas Holley Chivers

TUSAS 325

Thomas Holley Chivers

THOMAS HOLLEY CHIVERS

By CHARLES M. LOMBARD

University of Illinois
Chicago Circle

TWAYNE PUBLISHERS

A DIVISION OF G. K. HALL & CO., BOSTON

Published in 1979 by Twayne Publishers,
A Division of G. K. Hall & Co.
All Rights Reserved

Printed on permanent/durable acid-free paper and bound
in the United States of America

First Printing

Library of Congress Cataloging in Publication Data

Lombard, Charles M
Thomas Holley Chivers.

(Twayne's United States authors series; TUSAS 325)
Bibliography: p. 146-47
Includes index.
1. Chivers, Thomas Holley, 1809-1858
Criticism and interpretation.
PS1294.C4Z78   811'.3   78-12109
ISBN 0-8057-7258-8

Contents

About the Author

Charles Morris Lombard, the author of this study on Thomas Holley Chivers, did his graduate work in French at the University of Wisconsin where he received the doctorate in 1953. At present he is Professor of French at the University of Illinois, Chicago Circle. Professor Lombard has already published for TWAS studies of Lamartine, Joseph and Xavier de Maistre. He has written articles for various learned journals largely on the subject of early American interest in the French Romantics. In addition he has published at Gredos in Madrid, *French Romanticism on The Frontier,* a study of nineteenth century American interest in the French romantics.

Preface

Since his death over a century ago Thomas Holley Chivers has only on occasion been the subject of any serious study and has often been dismissed as a minor contemporary of Edgar Allan Poe whom he plagiarized at will. Some reputable scholars, among them S. Foster Damon, George Watts, and, to some extent, Jay B. Hubbell, admit that Poe was to varying degrees indebted to Chivers. What has not often been recognized is the influence of Swedenborg on Chivers. Ideas and imagery patently borrowed from the Swedish Theosophist are discussed in relation to their use by Chivers in adapting Swedenborgianism to his poetry, philosophy, and esthetics. Like other American writers before him, Jonathan Edwards and Ralph Waldo Emerson, Chivers perceived spiritual truths behind the material objects of the outer, physical world. During the period of Romanticism Swedenborg's theory of correspondences affected writers in the United States as well as Europe. In adopting a correspondential view of creation, Chivers stood hand in hand with Emerson, and shared with Poe a unique quality recognized in the latter by the French Symbolists.

Although one of the precursors of modern trends in poetry, Chivers was, as a man of his time, a typical Romantic. He wrote verse in a Byronic vein, praised America as a patriot, and as many a poet, before or since, spoke of unrequited love; inspired by Chateaubriand's *Atala* and *Les Natchez* he idealized the Indian and treated him with sympathy. Attracted to Black music and poetry he composed poems based on Black rhythms. He also had a deep attachment to the hymns and folk music of the white farmers in Georgia. Like Poe he experimented with the sound effects of words.

Reference is made to comments, favorable and unfavorable, on Chivers' works in order to assess his reputation both during his lifetime and after his death. Quotations are frequently rather lengthy owing to the relative unavailability of the Georgian's writings. The poet's lapses in grammar and spelling have been left unchanged so that the original text may not be unduly altered. Owing to limitations of space there is only a brief mention of minor volumes such as *The*

Path of Sorrow, Conrad and Eudora, Search After Truth, The Sons of Usna, and *Birthday Song of Liberty.*

The author wishes to thank Brown University Library for the opportunity to use its collection of Chivers' works and to express his gratitude to Duke University Library for granting him permission to consult its manuscript collection of Chivers' plays, essays, poems, and literary criticism.

CHARLES M. LOMBARD

Chicago Circle, Illinois

Chronology

1809 October 18, birth of Thomas Holley Chivers at Washington, Georgia.
1828 Enrolls at the Medical School of Transylvania University in Lexington, Kentucky.
1831 Begins exile away from home in despair over broken marriage.
1832 November 15, *Path of Sorrow*.
1833 *The Constitution of Man*.
1834 *Conrad and Eudora*.
1837 *Nacoochee*.
1845 *The Lost Pleiad*. In summer visits Poe in New York.
1848 *Search After Truth*.
1851 *Eonchs of Ruby*.
1853 "Origin of Poe's Raven" published July 23 starts Poe-Chivers Controversy. Writes *Atlanta, Memoralia, Virginalia*.
1856 *Birth-Day Song of Liberty*.
1857 Revises manuscript on Poe's life.
1858 *The Sons of Usna*. December 19, death of Chivers.

CHAPTER 1

Life of Chivers and Early Works

I Early Years

THOMAS Holley Chivers was born in Washington, Georgia, on October 18, 1809. His father, Colonel Robert Chivers, operated a prosperous mill and cotton farm. Georgia, early in the nineteenth century, had the vigor and energy of a young society. The first settlement at Savannah had been established in 1733, less than a century prior to Chivers birth. Indians, mainly the Creeks and Cherokees, while still a threat were located away from the Eastern coast in the West and Northwest of Georgia. In 1753 the territory became a royal colony, and, towards the end of the American Revolution, in 1780, the power of the British and Tories was broken. Warfare did not cease after the founding of the republic since there was always the danger of Indian raids.[1]

The decent citizens of Georgia were also troubled by reckless adventurers when the redskins were not on the warpath. Law and order were maintained by vigilantes and not professional police forces. In the midst of such turbulence the voice of protest was not stilled. Methodist and Baptist preachers denounced the immorality they saw about them in riotous living, gambling, drinking, and bordellos. When not joining forces against the common enemy of vice and corruption, Methodists and Baptists engaged in vigorous debates to prove which sect was the most Christian and scriptural in its teachings. Baptist ceremonies, more formal than those of their rivals, seemed devoid of life and color when compared to the spectacular revival meetings of the Methodists. Despite the frequent hair splitting on matters pertaining to theology and exegesis, both groups did agree that rebirth by faith and the salvation of the soul were central to Christian belief. The doctrine of an afterlife was comforting in a society where high mortality, particularly among children, existed, and funerals were one of the chief functions of the churches.[2]

During his days in Washington, Georgia, Chivers was oblivious to much of the turmoil and dynamism of the society in which he lived. Biographical details in his poems furnish a picture of a carefree lad who lived close to nature. Chivers never lost his affection for the family home which he later inherited. This attachment is explained in large part by a happy childhood spent at "Oaky Grove," a name he later gave to the home. Chivers always spoke of his father with respect, and frequently praised his mother in his poems.

II *Adolescence and Marriage*

Chivers was the oldest of three sons and four daughters. When one of his sisters, referred to as Adaline in later poems, died, Chivers witnessed her passing with considerable anguish. In recalling this first encounter with death Chivers told how, in the midst of his tribulations, the promise of eternal life had risen before him. After the loss of his sister, Chivers, had further unhappy experiences. In 1827 at the age of nineteen, he married a sixteen-year-old girl, Frances Elizabeth Chivers, a first cousin and the daughter of his father's brother, Joel. In less than a year Frances, even though already pregnant, left him. She never allowed Chivers to see his daughter, an indication that bitter feelings were at the root of their quarrel.[3]

Three years later in January, 1831, Chivers made a legal claim for Frances' portion of her father's estate and sued his mother-in-law, Elizabeth Chivers. When Thomas won the suit, Frances' mother promptly sued her daughter's husband in May, 1831, to obtain payment for his wife's board. Soon afterwards, Frances sued for divorce. Both suits against Chivers, by his wife and her mother, were dismissed by the court. Undaunted and still seeking revenge, Frances in March, 1821, sued Thomas for alimony on the grounds of cruelty and nonsupport of their child. By offering to take back his wife and child, Chivers was relieved by the court of any responsibility for them. In turn he tried unsuccessfully to divorce Frances in 1835. He blamed relatives for his wife's desertion, in particular, Franky Albert, the widow of an uncle, Thomas H. Chivers. He was not able to remarry apparently until he had found a loophole in Georgia law which invalidated the first marriage on the basis of the absence of the previous spouse for five years or more.

III *Sorrow Over Broken Marriage*

Chivers, who never forgave Frances, in his will left only one dollar to her and to his daughter. The years immediately following the quarrel and separation were painful ones for the impulsive Chivers. Spoiled by doting parents, he was poorly prepared for the taxing period of readjustment. Despite the loyalty of his immediate family there was evidently much local gossip about Chivers' abuse of his wife promulgated by Franky Albert. Unable to face this criticism though convinced of his innocence, Chivers left home. After entertaining for a moment a plan to leave America altogether, Chivers changed his mind and in 1828 enrolled in the medical program at Transylvania University in Lexington, Kentucky. Requirements were less stringent in those days, and, two years later in the spring of 1830, Chivers graduated with high honors. On March 17, 1830, he had submitted a thesis, entitled "Intermittent and Remittent Fevers," to the medical faculty at Transylvania.

While there, he composed poetry and eventually this avocation became his life's work. Medical studies at Transylvania, made a lasting impression on him and memories of his sister's passing intensified his preoccupation with death. Religious conventions then made the emphasis on a person's death fashionable, and an external manifestation of sorrow was deemed fitting and proper. What was common practice in the religious sphere also affected literary tastes. Poems, short stories, and novels written for popular consumption sold well if they featured deathbed scenes. Poetry on this very subject was to comprise a good part of Chivers' output. His knowledge of medicine enabled him to depict the last moments of the moribund graphically. By presentday standards, such an interest in death would be considered unduly morbid. Chivers took this theme seriously and treated the subject in all its grimness.

IV *Early Literary Efforts*

As a physician, Chivers is said to have practiced medicine for a brief period only to abandon it altogether. Still haunted by the memories of an unhappy marriage, he wandered about in the wilderness near Cincinnati and visited the Cherokee Indians. His movements in this period are difficult to trace. Poems, written in 1828-1829 were published in 1832 by the press of the *Weekly Review* in Franklin, Tennessee, under the title, *The Path of Sorrow,* or, *The Lament of Youth: A Poem.* Only a few copies of this work, of interest primarily for its autobiographic detail, survive.

Poetry was not the only literary form that attracted Chivers. Current interest in the theater led him to write a verse drama, *Conrad and Eudora,* published in 1834. The story concerned the Beauchamp-Sharpe murder case of the 1820's which came to be known as the Kentucky Tragedy. While at Transylvania, Chivers read a pamphlet, a confession by Jereboam O. Beauchamp, the murderer of Colonel Sharpe; he also must have met eye witnesses to the lurid courtroom trial that resulted in Beauchamp's execution. *Conrad and Eudora* was the first in a series of literary works based on the Kentucky Tragedy; in the same volume with the play, Chivers included a collection of poems, *Songs of the Heart.*

After having returned to Georgia in 1835, Chivers decided to concentrate on writing as a career. Already the author of some poetry and a tolerable drama, Chivers sent poems to the *Southern Literary Messenger* which refused to publish them. A stinging comment about the inferior verse submitted to the magazine by a "T. H. C., M.D." appeared on the editor's page, and some evidence indicates that these biting remarks came from the pen of Edgar Allan Poe. If so, it would mark the first indirect contact between the two writers. Other evidence also points to mutual borrowings from each other in the period 1835-1836.

A poem based on presumably authentic Indian legends was published in 1837 at Chivers' expense by W.E. Dean, a New York printer, under the title Nacoochee; *or, the Beautiful Star with Other Poems.* Of particular interest was the preface in which Chivers expounded some of his esthetic principles and his belief in the validity of dreams, visions, and a life beyond the grave. Chivers also revised *Conrad and Eudora* in 1838-1839 and gave the play a new title *Leoni; or, the Orphan of Venice.* This revision was probably made while he resided in New York. Subsequently, in 1839 he moved to Middletown, Connecticut, probably to please the charming Northerner, Harriett Hunt of Springfield, Massachusetts, whom Chivers on November 21, 1837, had married in New York.

The first eleven years of Chivers' marriage were marred by tragedy. His mother passed away on April 1, 1838. Four years later his favorite daughter, Allegra Florence Chivers, died on October 18, 1842. The final and most crushing blow was the death of his three

remaining children within a period of four months; Eugene Percy
Chivers, January 1848; Ada Lallage Chivers, April 2, 1848; Thomas
Holley Chivers, Jr., April 7, 1848. In subsequent poems Chivers
made frequent mention to them, especially of his mother and Allegra
Florence.

V *Chivers' Relations with Poe*

John Ostrom, in studying the Poe-Chivers correspondence, stated
that it covers a period of nine years. Many letters, although referred
to by both writers in existing letters, apparently were lost. According
to Ostrom, Poe wrote eight letters to Chivers which are now in
manuscript collections; there are two other letters Poe evidently sent
to Chivers but are as yet undiscovered. For his part Chivers sent
eleven known letters to Poe and in all probability at least fifteen
others, possibly more, that have still not been found.

In the first extant letter from Poe to Chivers the former seems bent
on soliciting money from the Georgian to underwrite a new journal,
the *Penn Magazine*. Financial aid, in fact, seems to be the dominant
theme in Poe's letters to Chivers with, at times, pathetic pleas for
immediate cash. It would appear that Poe considered Chivers a fair
poet although he also had an ulterior motive, the prospect of a loan,
when praising some of Chivers' inferior works. On August 29, 1845
Poe penned an urgent request to Chivers for fifty dollars at the time
he was preparing *The Raven and Other Poems* for publication. There
is no indication that Chivers actually sent any funds to Poe except for
the sum of five dollars and a half-hearted promise of an additional loan
of forty-five dollars.

In Poe's letter of August 29, 1845 there is evidence that Poe and
Chivers had met recently, since the former sends the best wishes of
his wife, Virginia, and mother-in-law, Mrs. Clemm. Chivers, in an
autograph copy of a letter he claimed to have received from Poe on
August 15, 1845, records the latter's regret that the Georgian thus far
had not yet visited him in New York. Emma Lester Chase and Lois
Ferry Parks, in their edition of Chivers' correspondence, feel the
Georgian was confused about the date of Poe's letter; evidence
available to them and other critics places the meeting of the two poets
in June, 1845. Richard Beale Davis in his edition of Chivers' *Life of
Poe* concludes the meeting could have taken place in June or July of
1845 when Poe, according to Chivers, accosted Lewis Gaylord Clark
rather belligerently in the street.

Chivers ostensibly avoided a second chance to see Poe in July, 1848 despite a pressing invitation from his fellow poet. Weary by now of Poe's begging, Chivers may have feared an unpleasant scene with the debt ridden writer. Chase and Parks conclude that Chivers may have offered hasty and unconvincing excuses for his failure to call on Poe, at Fordham in July, 1848 in an as yet undiscovered letter. Such a note might well be the "sneaking letter" from Chivers about which Poe complained to Mrs. Clemm on August 28-29 of 1849. The sensitive, irascible Georgian may have been offended by Poe's failure to accept an invitation to reside with him in Washington, Georgia. There, insisted Chivers, Poe would be provided with all necessary care and attention.

How long two such cantankerous individuals could have remained on peaceful terms on a day-to-day basis is an intriguing question but Chivers' offer does shed some light on his own reasons for cultivating Poe's friendship. From all appearances he took their relationship more seriously than the sophisticated Poe who knew his way around in Eastern literary circles with which Chivers, on the basis of available evidence, had little or no contact. To the Georgian the opportunity to have Poe as a permanent house guest would assure him an intelligent and engaging companion. In a leisurely and comfortable ambience they could continue their discussions on literature that began in New York in the summer of 1845. The frugal and pious Chivers would also be in a position to control Poe's spending, lecture him on the evils of drink (Chivers was a temperance crusader), and endeavor to convert him to Swedenborgianism. Poe's life style and agnosticism shocked Chivers whose reaction can be witnessed in a stern letter to Poe on September 24, 1844. In all probability Poe sensed the price he would have to pay for Chivers' hospitality and shuddered at the prospect. Far shrewder in business dealings than in his relations with hostile literary critics, Chivers, it would seem, quickly suspecting Poe's intention to ask continually for loans, apparently resorted to the invitation to reside with him as a mutually acceptable compromise. From this standpoint both poets had ulterior motives and it is, perhaps, regrettable Poe did not decide to live with Chivers. To the latter's credit he was a staunch defender of Poe after his death. Although he subsequently accused Poe of borrowing poetic themes and techniques from him he always acknowledged his colleague's greatness.

While Chivers and Poe were corresponding in the late 1840's, Americans were being attracted to the alleged supernatural manifestations that had been accomplished by Mesmerists and Spiritualists. *Poe's Eureka* in 1848 shows the influence of a well-known exponent of Spiritualism, Andrew Jackson Davis. In the same year Chivers published *Search After Truth; or, A New Revelation of the Psycho-Physiological Nature of Man*, a mixture of notions heavily colored with Swedenborg's teachings and a work designed to prove the immortality of the soul and to refute materialism. One positive result of Chivers' favorable attitude towards Spiritualism was that Davis' magazine, *The Univercoelum, or, Spiritual Philosopher*, published fourteen poems and three prose pieces by Chivers from 1848 to 1849. In addition, Chivers also succeeded in publishing poems in other reputable magazines such as *Graham's Broadway Journal*, and *Arthur's*.

VI   *Last Phase of Career*

Elated at seeing his cherished *Eonchs of Ruby* in print in 1850 Chivers expected fame as a reward for his efforts, not notoriety. Unfortunately in the minds of some critics the *Eonchs of Ruby* were a mediocre restatement of Poe's "The Raven" and "Ulalume." Pie, like Chivers, chose words devoid of easily recognizable meaning and in themselves beautiful and suggestive. The redeeming feature of Chivers' attitude in the controversy was a refusal to condemn Poe although convinced that the latter was the real plagiarist. In his manuscript, "A New Life of Edgar A. Poe," Chivers paid tribute to Poe's genius at a time when it was fashionable to excoriate the unfortunate author of *"The Raven."* Chivers had little use for Rufus Griswold and his coterie and seemed grateful to Poe for manifesting some degree of appreciation and friendship.

In the 1850's, when Chivers was spending much time up North, he had occasion to continue his work and to make arrangements to have three volumes of poetry published in 1853. *Virginalia* and *Memoralia* were printed in Philadelphia, and *Atlanta* in Macon, Georgia. Of the three works, *Virginalia* is highly regarded by some critics today along with *Atlanta*. Even *Memoralia* has some attractive selections.

Chivers' residence in the North was terminated in 1855. Perhaps the political climate produced by the rising tide of Abolitionism made him uneasy. After Chivers returned home the *Georgia Citizen* asked him to express his views about the political situation. Chivers lost no time in writing an article in which he advocated loyalty at the moment to the Union but foresaw the possibility of secession as the only way to preserve the integrity of Southern culture in the event Abolition won out. *Birth-Day Song of Liberty, A Paean of Glory for the Heroes of Freedom,* published in Atlanta in 1856, was nonetheless optimistic in tone and made no mention of secession.

After his return to the South, Chivers continued to publish his works, largely in the *Georgia Citizen.* Afflicted with a sudden illness Chivers wrote his will and died on December 18, 1858, at Decatur, Georgia, where he had moved from Washington two years before. His posthumous reputation was not confined to America. Some time after Chivers' death, Bayard Taylor, while on a visit to England, was surprised to hear Algernon Swinburne comment enthusiastically on the work of the idiosyncratic Georgian.

VII   *Chivers' Early Works*

Today there exist only a few copies of *The Path of Sorrow,* or, *The Lament of Youth: A Poem.* Chivers had his first collection of poetry published at his own expense in 1832 by the *Weekly Review* of Franklin, Tennessee. Many of the poems relate the events of Chivers' unfortunate marriage and criticize an unfaithful wife and a meddlesome relative, Franky Albert. Aside from autobiographic details, *The Path of Sorrow* has little artistic value. Chivers shows some interest in dreams and visions, a mystical aspect of his temperament that was more dramatically expressed in later works when under the influence of Swedenborg. Many of the poems in the volume are specimens of the current trends in magazine poetry.

The second of Chivers' works, *The Constitution of Man,* is known only through a five-page review article in *Western Monthly Magazine,* (1833), since there is no manuscript in existence today and no other journal seems to have reviewed it. From what can be ascertained in reading the review, *The Constitution of Man* was published in Memphis in 1833 as a twenty-two-page pamphlet, and was a theosophic exposition of man's nature and destiny in light of America's glorious future. Chivers' blend of illuminism and patriotism failed to impress the reviewer in *Western Monthly Magazine* (1833), who considered *The Constitution of Man* a bundle of absurdities.

After two inauspicious attempts to begin a literary career, Chivers put aside for the moment lyric poetry and philosophical treatises and in 1834, turned to the theater to write a melodrama, *Conrad and*

Eudora; or, The Death of Alonzo. A Tragedy. *In Five Acts. Founded on the Murder of Sharpe, by Beauchamp, in Kentucky.* (Poe based *Politian* on the same incident.) As the complete title indicates Chivers drew upon a contemporary subject, a murder trial in the 1820's that came to be known as the Kentucky Tragedy. Colonel Solomon P. Sharpe, a prominent politician, was stabbed to death on November 6, 1825, by Jereboam O. Beauchamp. The murderer was the husband of Sharpe's former mistress, Anne Cook, and he fancied himself the avenger of a lady's honor; in her early years Anne was actually little better than the local Jezebel. The trial became a cause célèbre since protection of a lady's reputation was supposedly the duty of a valiant gentleman. Moreover, there were rumors of political implications because of Sharpe's role in state politics.

Chivers had the opportunity at Transylvania University to acquire several pamphlets on the Kentucky Tragedy and probably to interview eye witnesses to the trial. Conrad and Eudora were ludicrous recreations of Jereboam and Anne in plotting the assassination of Alonzo who was a rather weak caricature of Colonel Sharpe; the play itself was unhappily just another turgid and outlandish closet drama that was never staged. Its only claim to distinction was that of being the first work on the theme of the Kentucky Tragedy. Other plays concerned with Sharpe's murder were to follow. The best of them was Poe's *Politian* (1835) which, though far superior in style to *Conrad and Eudora*, was too unwieldy to present upon the stage. Not until Robert Penn Warren's *World Enough and Time* (1950) did the subject of Sharpe and Beauchamp result in a work of substantial literary merit.

Published in the same volume with *Conrad and Eudora* was a collection of forty-nine poems under the title "Songs of the Heart." Largely a rehash of *The Path of Sorrow*, Chivers produced a similar assortment of inconsequential love lyrics and pseudo-Byronic outbursts of personal frustration. There was no indication that the writer of such trivia would at any future time be judged an innovator of new poetic techniques and motifs.

CHAPTER 2

Chivers' Interest in the American Indian and Swedenborg

I *Chateaubriand and the Idealized Indian*

NOT too long ago Howard Mumford Jones conceded that the "ideality of Chateaubriand" was a significant factor in the formation of American Romanticism.[1] Early in the nineteenth century French writers were widely read in America before German authors had much influence on the budding literature of the United States. Federalist distrust of French culture at the turn of the century discouraged any interest in Voltaire and in the rationalists of the Enlightenment. However, *Paul et Virginie* by Bernardin de Saint Pierre and Rousseau's *La Nouvelle Héloïse,* were popular in the 1790's and 1800's. Chauteaubriand, in the period of the Second Great Awakening (c. 1795-1834) was considered their successor by Protestants who, terrified by Deism, turned to the writings of a Catholic apologist and welcomed the defense of Christianity in the *Génie du Christianisme* and *Atala.* Both works were available in French and English translation on the Eastern seaboard before the War of 1812.

When in Paris in 1817, the young George Ticknor made it a point to visit Chateaubriand and to enjoy the melancholy writer's rhetorical powers. Another New Englander, Ralph Waldo Emerson, in his reading also took note of Chateaubriand but, disregarding the French writer's philosophical speculations, concentrated instead on his language and imagery.[3] As is often the case, now forgotten figures were the most enthusiastic in drawing on Chateaubriand in their own writings. One author on the then frontier was unrestrained in his enthusiasm. A grouchy preacher, Timothy Flint, hostile to the Eastern literary establishment and eager to promote a native literature in the West, encouraged the study of Chateaubriand in preference to cultural subservience to England. To publicize his views on literature, he founded the *Western Monthly Review* (1827-1830) in Cincinnati where he had ample opportunity to acquaint subscribers with *Atala*. Flint insisted Chateaubriand had been profoundly affected by his stay in America with the Indians and that the distinctive "mental coloring" in the style and language of *Atala* was attributable to the Frenchman's lasting impressions of the vast wilderness of the New World.[4]

Atala captured not only the imagination of creative writers but appealed as well to serious students of Indian life. Henry R. Schoolcraft (1793-1864) read Chateaubriand's idyl during a bitterly cold winter in Northern Michigan in 1821 when surrounded by potentially hostile Chippewas; later he composed *Ahallo*, a poem, modeled on *Atala*. An associate of Schoolcraft's, Henry Whiting (1788-1851), a military man with extensive knowledge of the redman, became the unlikely author of *Ontwa* (1822) and *Sanillac* (1831), two narrative poems idealizing the Indian. By Whiting's own admission, *Atala* strongly affected the tone and coloring of his works. Lewis Cass, governor of the Michigan territory, was frequently assisted in the supervision of Indian affairs by Schoolcraft and Whiting. Their works on the American aborigine, especially those of Whiting, were commended by Cass, an admirer of French literature, who must have recognized the effect of *Atala* upon the writings of his two associates.[5]

The story line of Chateaubriand's tale is clear and uncomplicated. Chactas, an old Indian chief, meets René, a melancholy young Frenchman who came to America to forget an unnatural love for his sister, Amélie. The scene is set in Louisiana when the territory was still a French colony. Chactas, reared by Lopez, an old Spaniard, is rescued from the savage Muscogulges by a beautiful Indian maid, Atala. A Christian, she leads Chactas to a village inhabited by other converts. There the missionary, Père Aubry, lectures Chactas on Christianity. Atala and Chactas spend many happy moments together amid the splendor of the unspoiled forests. When Chactas becomes too passionate in his declarations of love, Atala, adhering to her vow to remain a virgin, commits suicide. After her burial, Chactas sadly takes leaves of Père Aubry. The subsequent adventures of Chactas and René are related in *Les Natchez*. Both meet their death at the hands of hostile Indians. Written in majestic French prose *Atala*, even in pedestrian English translations, had a strong appeal to American readers of the Romantic period. *Les Natchez* also enjoyed considerable popularity in America but *Atala* was so widely imitated by American writers that poems or plays based on the Atala theme became a fad among Romantic authors in the United States. A comely Indian lass, thoroughly Christianized and speaking a refined poetic language, was invariably the sweetheart of a stalwart handsome brave patterned after Chactas. Invariably their love affair had a tragic end.

On stage in the 1820's and 30's appeared a number of plays about the noble savage patterned after *Atala* and *Les Natchez*. Among them were Lewis F. Thomas' *Osceola;* Caroline L. Hentz's *Lamorah;* Alexander MaComb's *Pontiac;* Robert D. Owens' *Pocahontas;* Robert M. Bird's *Oralloosa; Outalissi* by an anonymous author, represents a clear borrowing from *Les Natchez.* Outalissi was the father of Chactas.[6]

Two other novelists who capitalized on the Indian, James Fenimore Cooper and Robert M. Bird, publicly rejected any charges of imitating Chateaubriand. His protests notwithstanding, Robert M. Bird's novels, as well as his play *Oralloosa,* captured the spirit of Chateaubriand. The case against James Fenimore Cooper is much stronger. Chingachgook and Hawkeye recall the comradeship of Chactas and René. Moreover, Cooper had great admiration for Chateaubriand; and, even though evidence indicates he read little if any of the Frenchman's writings, he was reared in a cultural milieu where *Atala* would be a frequent topic of conversation.[7]

Poe was certainly no stranger to French Romanticism and especially to Chateaubriand. The excessive sentimentalism of *Atala* and *Les Natchez* was unpalatable to Poe who appreciated, nonetheless, the beauty of Chateaubriand's prose. Passages in Poe's "To Zante" paraphrase lines from *Itinéraire de Paris à Jerusalem* while a souvenir of the *Génie du Christianisme* may be read in "The Bells." "What a tale of terror, now, their turbulency tells."[8] Chateaubriand emphasized the manner in which the tolling of bells was often associated with impending disaster.

The *New Yorker* of 1836 printed a saccharine specimen of doggerel in honor of the author of *Atala* that summarized the sentiments of American writers of the Chateaubriand school. "The sire of Atala, pale child of Sorrow. / Painter of Chactas' faith and René's gloom, / Who from Hope's blasted flower no balm could borrow, / And longed to burst the portal of the tomb."[9] Nor was mention of Chateaubriand limited to ham poetry. His name could pop up in the most unlikely spots. The locale of *The Southwest* (1835), one of many blood curdling, dime novels by Joseph Holt Ingraham, is Fort Rosalie, the main scene of *Les Natchez*. Quite willing to disclose the source of his inspiration, Ingraham obsequiously quotes six pages from Chateaubriand's novel.[10] Sober students of French literature in America in the 1840's continued to emphasize the moral value of Chateaubriand, a quality then considered rare in French writers. Moreover, he was studied earnestly by scholars interested in the Indian. Francis Parkman read him intently and George Bancroft considered *Les Natchez* a valuable source of information on the redman.[11]

Among the literary salons that arose in New York in the 1840's, one of the most popular among literati and francophiles was that of Anne Lynch Botta; the hostess was a good friend of Poe and attracted to her parlors Caroline M. Kirkland, Julia W. Howe, and the sedate critic, Henry T. Tuckerman. Frequent guests included Emerson, George Ripley, and other prominent names in the literary and artistic world. Most of the habitués of Anne's drawingroom admired some aspect of Chateaubriand.[12] The list of Anne's guests may even have included Chivers. If so, he would have agreed with those in attendance only on the merits of *Atala,* for the Georgian was generally hostile to the literati.

In view of the popularity of *Atala* and *Les Natchez* and the subsequent development of a substantial body of literature that idealized the Indian, Longfellow's *Hiawatha* (1855) appears as the logical culmination of a trend in American letters that persisted for several decades. The meter of Longfellow's poem might well be Finnish in origin, but Hiawatha and Minnehaha possess several traits in common with Chactas and Atala. As the first well-known American poet to have a wide knowledge of continental literature, Longfellow, like his fellow writers, was attracted to Chateaubriand. The general outlines of the description of the American wilderness in *Atala* and *Les Natchez* are recalled by the preface to *Evangeline.* Even the priest in Longfellow's poem about the Acadians seems a close relative to Père Aubry. Thirty years before the publication of the *Song of Hiawatha* Longfellow was still quoting *Atala* about the oblivion into which a person enters after death. Unlike the primitive *Kalevala,* of unknown authorship, *Hiawatha* is a relatively refined poem more pastoral in tone when the Finnish epic and with few scenes of violence.[13]

Henry R. Schoolcraft wrote to Longfellow in 1855 and noted that

"from the days of 'Atala'" there had been a question among
American writers concerning the extent to which "Indian character
and mythology are material for poetry."[14] Schoolcraft himself had
attempted to recapitulate the Atala theme in *Ahallo*, an effort that
proved him to be a better anthropologist than a poet. What is of
more importance, however, is that, in Schoolcraft's mind, Longfellow marked a continuation of the Chateaubriand trend in American
letters; there was substantial justification for Schoolcraft's assumption. *Hiawatha*, like *Atala*, has elements suceptible of a Christian
interpretation. Although Hiawatha's world is inhabited by good and
bad spirits, he and Minnehaha on the whole act with the restraint
American readers of the nineteenth century would associate with
high-minded Christians. By comparison, Longfellow's Indians are
more realistic than Chateaubriand's; but the American poet profited from the artistic interpretation provided by his French colleague. The *Song of Hiawatha* is the culmination of a trend started
by Chateaubriand and, with the exception of Chivers' Indian
poems, was the only significant effort by a poet of any stature.
Confined almost entirely to secondary writers, the Atala fad was
symptomatic of the period like so many other subcurrents in literary history. Young authors, anxious to break ties with England and
develop a new literature based on native material, turned to a
French writer who had written a successful work on a distinctly
American theme.

II *Sources on the Indian Used by Chivers*

How then does Chivers fit into the picture of American interest in
the noble Indians of Chateaubriand? In the first place he had the
same exposure to French literature as Poe and other Southern
gentlemen. He in all probability read *Atala* and *Les Natchez* and must
have been familiar with Flint, Whiting, and other writers in the
Chateaubriand vein. An inveterate theatergoer, Chivers undoubtedly saw several plays in the East in which dignified stage Indians
expressed their wise and stoical philosophy. In literary reviews, he
doubtless read articles about Chateaubriand together with poems
and stories on themes takes from *Atala* and *Les Natchez*. Among the
papers of S. Foster Damon at the library of Brown University are
notes on Chivers' reading of Chateaubriand.

In *Atala*, Chivers found the material for several poems on the
Christianized Indian maid who lifts her voice in prayer to Jesus.

There are also the passages describing Atala's death and her rescue of Chactas that provided useful material to Chivers. In *Les Natchez* the main plot centers around the romance and marriage of Celuta and René who is adopted by the Natchez. Their connubial bliss is complicated by Onduré's lecherous designs on Celuta and by Mila whose amourous conduct towards René makes trouble for all concerned; her coy remarks about René in Celuta's presence arouse the latter's jealousy and suspicions. At one point in *Les Natchez*, René describes an island in the middle of a lake in Florida where a fountain of youth is located. When René is a prisoner of the Illini, he is visited by an Indian girl Nelida, *la Vièrge des dernieres amours*, or, as then commonly translated into English—by the "Virgin of the First Fond Love." Chivers adapted all the foregoing names and incidents to his own plays and poetry.[15]

Chateaubriand was not the only source on the Indian used by Chivers. "The Chickamauga Indian's Conversion" has direct references to James Adair's *History of American Indians* and to William Bartram's *Travels*.[16] Adair described the Achi-Magus, or venerable seer, and drew many parallels between the early Jews and the "red Hebrews." The Indians, according to Adair, had statues resembling cherubims and a belief in the "ministration of angels" or good spirits.[17] Bartram in his itinerary related how he met a slave girl among the Choctaws. She had recently been made a captive and was suffering from homesickness after hearing songs of her homeland sung by a young passerby. Bartram also encountered a white trader with a beautiful Seminole wife; like Adair, he noted the Indian belief in a "world of souls." Conchshells, used as a frequent symbol by Chivers, were described by Bartram who saw them utilized by the Indians as ceremonial drinking cups and as a horn by an overseer to assemble tribesmen in the town square before repairing to the fields to till the soil.[18]

Quite a few Indian names and terms employed by Chivers were direct borrowings from the French writer: Areskoui, the evil spirit; Michabon, the spirit of the waters; Outalissi, father of Chactas; Outougamiz, brother of Chactas; Lopez, Atala's father and René's benefactor; Simaghan, chief of the Muscogulges and Atala's stepfather. Chivers also referred to Indian ceremonies and customs mentioned by Chateaubriand in *Atala* and *Les Natchez:* the Feast of Death; the Festival of Souls; the Banqueting of Souls; the Land of Souls; the Isle of Souls.[19]

Aside from Chateaubriand, Chivers looked elsewhere for ter-

minology and incidents to use in his works on the Indian. A main
character in his poems and plays is Julian, a popular name in
nineteenth-century Romanticism and one used by Walter Scott in
Vision of Don Roderick and by William S. Landor in *Count Julian*.
René's role as the European living among the Indians is taken over by
Julian in Chivers' writings. Like René in *Les Natchez*, Julian in
Atlanta is seated at one point near a cavern.

During his childhood, Chivers heard accounts of the Indians and
gathered information about their folklore. The data he collected
consist of authentic legends of the redman or stories fabricated by
Europeans in which a literary formula is imposed on a primitive
culture.[20] *Nacoochee, or the Evening Star*, exemplifies this
Europeanization of Indian legends. The term "Nacoochee" is derived
from the Cherokee language and has been used to name a village, a
valley, and a mound in Georgia. White men have composed their own
mythology about this region and the mound in which Nacoochee
becomes a beautiful princess enamored of the handsome chief of a
rival tribe; the two lovers meet in secret until discovered by the girl's
father. In one adaptation, they are both slain by the old chief's braves;
in another, they hurl themselves from a cliff into the turbulent waters
below. Grief stricken, Nacoochee's father orders a mound built on
the spot where the two lovers used to meet.[21] The "death leap" and
the Romeo-Juliet theme are too readily identifiable with European
Romanticism and possess no elements in common with Indian
mythology. In aboriginal folklore the story of the maid and her lover is
seldom found; and, when it does occur, it is more common among the
plains Indians than the Georgia tribes familiar to Chivers. Primitive
cultures, in general, follow what is, by comparison to Romantic
themes, a rather rigid and complicated pattern of social conduct.
Only one known Cherokee myth involves a boy and girl, but it
concerns a brother and sister. He mourns her death and goes to the
land of spirits to bring her back to earth.[22]

Another narrative device used by Chivers is also derived from the
white man's literary tradition. In his works, *Count Julian* and
Atlanta, the hero disguises himself as the chief's dead son in order to
trick the old man. Deception by disguise does occur in folk tales and
certain Indian tribes had the practice of having living persons
impersonate departed souls in rituals for the dead.[23] The episode in
Chivers' works differs from Indian customs and involves impersona-
tion of a specific individual in order to hoodwink an old Indian and

gain his confidence, a trick which recalls the biblical account of Esau and Jacob.

A further example of the European tendency to adapt Indian tradition to Continental culture can be seen in the Georgian's use of names derived from Macpherson's alleged translation of the Gaelic bard, Ossian. Chivers uses Ossianic names, Lena and Selma, and frequently calls his Indian chiefs "Lamorah" a popular name with American Romantics. *Lamora* is a title of a poem attributed to Ossian and translated by Baron Edmund de Harold, and a Sir Lamorak was one of the knights of the Round Table.[24] The justification for applying Celtic names to Indians is explainable not only in light of Ossian's popularity in the era of Romanticism but also by widespread belief in the "Welsh theory." According to this hypothesis, based on Lloyd's *History of Cambria* (1584), Welsh bards related how Prince Madoc of Wales sailed Westward in 1170 and discovered new lands. On his return he sent out another expedition that never came back. Presumably the Welsh explorers settled among the Indians. During the eighteenth century there were several reports of Indians who spoke a language closely resembling Welsh. A Rev. Morgan Jones supposedly escaped death when Indian marauders heard him pray in Welsh, a tongue they recognized as their own. Serious linguistic research has thoroughly discredited the "Welsh theory." The only European words in Indian languages originate from the early days of colonization.[25]

The result of fanciful theories about the origin of native Americans was a Europeanized aborigine who often sounded more like an Ossianic warrior than a full-blooded Indian. Chieftains, named Lamorah or Selma, mouthed clichés reminiscent of Chateaubriand and Macpherson. One egregious error was to portray an Indian woman with the bearing, manner, and language of a princess from the continent. An examination of Colonial records reveals that the hardy squaws had their own peculiar status; and, for women in a primitive society, had a certain degree of freedom from male chauvinism. The Iroquois would not go to war without first consulting their women. Many a war party owed its success in the field to squaws who formed a supply corps behind the battle line and provided such necessities as food and medicine.[26]

Chivers followed the prevailing trend of idealizing the Indians, but he occasionally portrayed them as impulsive aborigines ready to kill and scalp the enemy. Even Chateaubriand did not overlook the

violent side of the Indian temperament. A certain number of Indian
names and terms used by Chivers were reasonably accurate. Along
with Nacoochee, the name of Ostenee is also Cherokee and derives
from Ostonoos, a village.[27] Chivers in his works on the Indians
interpolated some rather authentic data taken from their mythology.
Enchanted lakes, magic caves, and spirits returned from the dead
were all featured in the folklore of the Cherokees and their neighbor-
ing tribes. Chivers was equally factual when writing about the
Seminoles, and from Samuel G. Drake's *Chronicles of the Indians*
obtained details of the Seminole War and its principal figures and
events for his play *Osceola*.[28]

III   *Chivers' Use of the Indian Theme*

"Atala's Prayer," one of Chivers' better poems on the Indian
theme, received special praise from Poe. *Malavolti, Nacoochee,* and
Atlanta are longer, narrative poems with variations on the tale of the
Indian maid and her lover. Malavolti is the white lover untrue to the
Indian maid; but the tables are turned in *Nacoochee* when Ostenee
sees the object of his desires snatched away by an angel. In *Atlanta*,
Julian, disguised as Lamorah's son, Yanessa, outwits the old chief and
saves Ianthe from the villainous Ostenee. *Count Julian*, begins like
Atlanta, with Julian's tricking the old chief into accepting him as his
son in order to reach his beloved; but the play is soon bogged down
with names and incidents borrowed from *Atala* and *Les Natchez*.

In most of Chivers' Indian plays and poems, the main action
involves a slave girl, an idea suggested by the captive maiden
described by Bartram and by the story of *Atala*. In *Nacoochee* and in
Atlanta, the maiden dwells on an enchanted island in the middle of a
lake. Such an isle, supposedly located in Florida, is described by
René in *Les Natchez* and is also the basis of a Cherokee legend.[29]
However, Chateaubriand's works, more refined and poetic in conception, still remain the principal source of *Nacoochee* and *Atlanta*.

The myths of the Cherokees, which Chivers most likely knew by
word of mouth, cannot be disregarded. In Cherokee theology the
river was an important symbol of life and death; and, according to
Cherokee belief, there were seven upper worlds or heavens to which
Cherokees could aspire while the priest prayed. If the omens were
good and a Cherokee raised his mind to the seventh level, he attained
eternal life.[30] Chivers may have been struck by certain parallels
between Indian beliefs and those of Christianity. In this respect, he

was like Adair who observed that both the early Hebrews and the Indians had a holy place or temple and believed in the intercession of good spirits or angels.

At the same time early Romantics were modeling their works on *Atala* and *Les Natchez,* some critics protested against the heavy emphasis on Frenchified Indians. One critic in the *New York Mirror* (1837) reprimanded Chivers, "Our author must have copied his costume from some French illustration of Chateaubriand's Indian Romance."[31] Such criticism, as was usually the case, undoubtedly infuriated Chivers and only served to strengthen his determination to compose additional plays and poems about Indian life.

IV   *Chivers and Swedenborg*

Among Chiver's unpublished manuscripts in the Duke University Library there are several references to concepts patently borrowed from Swedenborg as well as direct mention of the Swedish theologian. In "Philosophic Marginalia" he expresses gratitude for having received from an unnamed friend a "pamphlet and the leaves from Swedenborg," and in the "Essay on Love" there is a statement to the effect that for Swedenborg faith and truth are one and the same. Even without a direct reference to Swedenborg Chivers' borrowings from him are unmistakable in view of the evidence that the Georgian poet took ideas time and again directly from the Scandinavian mystic. Swedenborgian terminology is used freely by Chivers in speaking of the theory of correspondences, celestial love, the material and spiritual bodies, and angelic presences. Undoubtedly Chivers read at the very least portions of Swedenborg's *Arcana Coelestia.*

The religious thought of Swedenborg furnished many ideas that formed the basis of Chivers' esthetics and provided as well themes incorporated into his poetry. In this section an outline is given of some major points in Swedenborg's system that appealed to Chivers.

Man, in the theology of the Swedenborgian mystic, is only a step away from eternal life, possessing as he does two bodies, the one material and the other spiritual. In the first phase of man's life on earth he wears a material body in which he lives and acts on the terrestial plane. During this period, man, through his actions, determines his ultimate destiny, be it heaven or hell. Death separates man from his material body. The spiritual body remains and man continues to live in a world as real as the one he has left; this new world is composed of a spiritual substance; here man lives forever through the sustaining power of God. By this theory Swedenborg explained and justified his contact with the spirit world into which he claimed to be able to pass at will. In fact, Swedenborg insisted that the material and spiritual worlds resembled each other so closely that only by reflecting upon his situation did he realize in which sphere, material or spiritual, he actually happened at a particular moment to be.

In Swedenborg's system there is no sudden and drastic change in a person's situation after death. Awareness of life in the material sphere is merely exchanged for consciousness of existence in the spiritual order. Society continues in heaven as it is known on earth with similar social structures and institutions. There is marriage in heaven for man and woman are intended to complement each other in body and spirit; only now it is a union of minds with an absence of carnal pleasure. When this type of union already exists in the material world it is transferred to the spiritual realm where a higher degree of perfection is realized. Although a man may not be married to a woman on earth he can in a spiritual way become associated with a person having the same temperament and character.

A central theme in Swedenborg's thinking that deeply affected Chivers is the glorified state enjoyed by mankind in Paradise; in *Search After Truth* Chivers called this state "Edenic." Adam fell, according to Swedenborg, from a level of perfection to which he had been raised through a lengthy spiritual education. Primitive man was well intentioned but possessed only rudimentary concepts and emotions. For a while, man, in the initial period of his spiritual development, made considerable progress for he accepted instinctively all divine truths presented to him. This ideal condition continued for some time; man could even converse with angels. A choice of good or evil had to be made before man could pass into the World of Spirits. The decline of man from this level achieved in Eden was gradual and reached the point where the sensuous side of man asserted itself. As a result of the fall man did not stop loving God and neighbor but mistakenly assumed that virtues he possessed were of his own making.

Swedenborg, in breaking with older schools of Christian theology, taught that God was ultimately the Divine Man. In order to discover some purpose in the universe and to justify his own system, Swedenborg tried to explain how everything in the material world, no matter how imperfectly, had to correspond to God. The Creator was thus a perfect reflection of an imperfect world; all truths, spiritual and material, corresponded to him.

Another engrossing aspect of Swedenborg's teaching is the emphasis on love as an enduring emotion and not an ephemeral mood. To Swedenborg love constituted the substance of the mind and was the basis for its process. God's substance itself was Divine Love. A prime example of the proper expression of love was wisdom, for the quality of human love could be developed and expanded until it was truly universal.

So convinced was Swedenborg about the pervasiveness of God's power that he did not consider life itself to be a quality inherent in man. An effect, to Swedenborg's way of thinking, could endure only as long as the cause was present. Since immortality was not an essential human attribute, man had to depend constantly on the influx of divine life. All creation, good and evil, received this divine influx.

On the subject of the Word, taken as God's revelation, Swedenborg maintained that it had both a spiritual and a material meaning. Man acquires knowledge gradually in his natural life, and afterwards, in the World of Spirits, he seeks a higher degree of perfection. In heaven, as conceived by Swedenborg, there were three levels: the spiritual, or middle heaven; the celestial, or highest; and the lowest, the spiritual-natural. Man, in the process of acquiring divine truth, passes successively through these three stages. As he progresses, he becomes increasingly aware of the spiritual truths behind the material forms of the physical world.

The intimate connection between the material and spiritual orders was always stressed by Swedenborg. Physical objects were created by spiritual causes and any traits possessed by these objects were traceable to these very causes. Man's intelligence was capable of expressing these relationships in symbols. Since no human mind was isolated in this life, it could have contact with other minds, not only on a material plane but on a spiritual one as well. Properly inspired, human thoughts could contact even angelic minds.

Many of Swedenborg's conclusions, such as the teachings on angels and the material and spiritual orders, were derived from his highly allegorical interpretations of Scripture and his effort to bring them up to date in accordance with his own theological outlook. He envisioned a new heaven and earth that had no connection whatsoever with the physical universe. The old heaven and earth would remain and their new counterparts would be the rejuvenated internal and external states of the human mind.

Quite a few of the principles briefly outlined above affected Chivers' views on esthetics and choice of themes in his poetry. The Swedenborgian precept of the constant influx of divine life was stressed by Chivers as an essential element in poetic inspiration. The Georgian's frequent emphasis on poets as lovers of beauty recalls Swedenborg's teaching about love as the substance of the mind. Chivers' love lyrics often seem a reflection of the notion that the bond between man and woman, once begun in the material world, was to be perfected and sublimated in the spiritual sphere. He alludes more than once in his works to the spiritual and material bodies and in the functions of the spiritual body Chivers finds the faculties that, as a poet, empower him to perceive eternal verities. His pursuit of a higher reality is facilitated by the theory of correspondences which enable him to discover the spiritual order beyond the physical world. As a believer, Chivers wishes to have an intimate vision of God, the Divine Man, the object of all true poets in his estimation. Preoccupied with the belief that he can contact angelic minds, Chivers often senses the presence of angels and has visions of the return of departed loved ones. In narrative poems like *Malavolti*, *Nacoochee*, and *Atlanta*, Chivers envisages an ideal woman who in this life already prepares for a spiritual union with God or a suitable mate in heaven. Perhaps the most unique feature of Chivers' interest in Swedenborg was his effort to produce striking impressions of sound and color through unusual imagery used in his poems; it represented an earnest attempt by Chivers to impart to the reader a vivid, albeit indirect, sensation of the spiritual world linked correspondentially to the material world known to man.

V   *American Interest in the Theory of Correspondences*

The American theologian, Jonathan Edwards (1703-1758) was probably the first writer of note in America to make use of a symbolism that recognized a dual principle in the universe, namely that a specific material object could signify a deeper spiritual truth. In his writings on the Apocalypse Edwards frequently alluded to the meaning of the imagery and symbolism in the Revelation to John. Despite the stern Calvinistic tone of his prose he was capable, as indicated by his comments, of considerable response and sensitivity to the literary aspects of the Apocalypse.

Green, to Edwards, "being a most pleasing color was a fit symbol of grace and mercy" in the Apocalypse. Red had a far-reaching signification to him inasmuch as "turning the third part of the sea into blood" meant "the empire's losing of whole states." A substance like water could have two quite different interpretations, either as "the emblem of instability" or, when considered in tremendous volume, "waters and rivers in scripture language. . . meant supplies of any city or kingdom . . . their wealth and treasures." As for mathematical symbolism, the number "seven" was "everywhere put for perfection . . . because in seven days all things were perfected and completed."[32]

Edwards, in acknowledging an interrelationship of the material and spiritual orders, anticipated Swedenborg's notions on correspondences as applied by later American writers. Swedenborgianism officially became a part of the religious scene here with the arrival of James Glen in Philadelphia during the summer of 1784 to spread the teachings of the New Church. Not long after Glen's coming the works of Swedenborg were shipped to America to appear in libraries of the New Church established in Pennsylvania, Virginia, and Kentucky. By the 1790's the New Church had followers throughout the South and the writings of Swedenborg could also be found in several private libraries. In New York a Swedenborgian society was formed. One of its members was the poet Samuel Woodworth[33] (1784-1842), author of "The Old Oaken Bucket." While a minor poet Woodworth on occasion could perceive the universe in correspondential terms worthy of his Swedenborgian background. One poem appropriately entitled "Philosophy and Religion" (1818) explains the complexity of creation by the theory of correspondences: "And there is a philosophy truly divine / That traces effects up to spiritual causes / Determines the link of the chain where they join, / And soars to an infinite height ere it pauses. - - -   - - - -   - - -   --   Hail, science of Angels! Theosophy, hail! / That shows us the regions of bliss by reflection, / Removes from Creation's broad mirror the veil, / Where spirit and matter appear in connection."[34]

Dull and didactic lines perhaps, but Woodworth does provide an early example in nineteenth-century American poetry of a recognition of the correspondential aspects of the universe. His study of Swedenborg led him to edit two journals under the auspices of the New Church, the *Halcyon Luminary* (1812-13) and the *New Jerusalem Missionary* (1823-24).[35] Woodworth enjoyed more public attention in his lifetime then Chivers owing to the popularity of

poems like "The Old Oaken Bucket" and "The Hunters of Kentucky."
He also had some success in the theater.

Trouble began for orthodox Swedenborgians when spiritualists
claimed Swedenborg as one of their own and interpreted the *Arcana
Coelestia* freely and without restraint to the horror of sober theolo-
gians of the New Church. The crisis climaxed in the 1840's with the
revelations of an untutored cobbler from Poughkeepsie, Andrew
Jackson Davis (1826-1910). On November 28, 1845, Davis while in a
trance began to dictate his *Principles of Nature* and finished it on
January 25, 1847. The work was a mixture of ideas borrowed from
Swedenborg and Fourier. Swedenborgians and nonSwedenborgians
alike attacked the work. A scholar of the New Church, George Bush
(1796-1859), at first took the uninstructed Davis seriously and
credited him with a valid power of mediumship or contact with
departed spirits. Not quite certain that Davis actually conversed with
the spirit of Swedenborg, Bush did testify to the cobbler's ability to
quote at length from the *Arcana Coelestia* in Latin and Greek. One of
Bush's preoccupations was to associate Swedenborg's principles with
mesmerism; in 1847 he published a book *Mesmer and Swedenborg* to
prove the connection. Pressure from conservatives in the New
Church obliged Bush to recant his errors shortly afterwards.[36]
Chivers was acquainted with Bush and the two men maintained an
intermittent correspondence from 1849 to 1858.[37] Given the Georgian's preoccupation with dreams, ghostly apparitions, and contact
with the spirit world he might have been encouraged in his beliefs by
Bush's comments on the alleged mediumship of Davis.

Not inclined in the least to accept the claims of Spiritualists, Ralph
Waldo Emerson, nonetheless, had more than a passing interest in
Swedenborg, who "led the most real life of any man then in the
world." To Emerson in *Swedenborg, or the Mystic* (1845) the Swedish
seer was a remarkable individual capable of profound intellectual
speculations but without a poetic bent. Overly involved in theology
Swedenborg failed to elucidate sufficiently the theory of correspondences. As a result, Emerson lamented: ". . . Down to this hour,
literature has no book in which the symbolism of things is scien-
tifically opened."[38]

The celebrated trances of Swedenborg were to Emerson attributable to a psychotic state of mind. "A certain tendency to insanity has
always attended the opening of the religious sense in men . . . the
illuminations of Swedenborg are of this kind."[39] Emerson's use of the
term "insanity" was in no wise derogatory since he credited Sweden-

borg with the unceasing examination of "the double meaning . . . of every sensuous fact." The New England writer's admiration for the Scandinavian mystic was unquestionable to the point that the essay *Nature* (1836) was mistaken by many for a New Church work and for good reason.[40] *Nature* is replete with Swedenborgian notions that Emerson seems to find intensely poetic despite his disapproval of Swedenborg's unpoetic temperament.

"Particular natural facts are symbols of particular spiritual facts," Emerson asserts in *Language* (1836), thus anticipating Chivers' later vehement statements on the theory of correspondences as a source of rich, poetic material. "Outer Creation" was the language for "inward creation." With this principle in mind Emerson stresses the concept of correspondences still further: "Every natural fact is a symbol of some spiritual fact. Every appearance in nature corresponds to some state of mind."[41] Chivers, in view of the initial public impression that *Nature* was a New Church tract, might well have read Emerson seriously and carefully as a Swedenborgian authority.

Other notions subsequently expressed by Chivers in *Search After Truth* and the prefaces to his various volumes of poetry may also be found in *Language*. These ideas in a sense had long been Romantic commonplaces derived from the Schlegels and Novalis (Freiherr von Hardenberg) and ultimately Jakob Behmen (Emerson ranked Behmen with Swedenborg as one of the great intuitive geniuses.) Prior to Chivers Emerson emphasized poetry as the natural form of expression used by men in primitive times: "As we go back in history, language becomes more picturesque, until its infancy, when it is all poetry." Almost as though he were adhering to a Chiversian formula Emerson traces the decline of the spoken word: "The corruption of man is followed by the corruption of language." To accomplish the restoration of language to a state akin to its pristine purity the one who employed it had to be "a man in alliance with truth and God."[42]

While not burdened with Chivers' complicated notions on New Church metaphysics and mysticism, Emerson conceded in *Prospects* (1836) that some form of spiritual rejuvenation was needed for an esthetic renaissance; "The problem of restoring to the world original and eternal beauty is solved by the redemption of the soul."[43] Chivers would be in fundamental agreement with Emerson on many points, namely, Swedenborg's correspondential view of the universe, the poetry of primitive language, and the factors required for a linguistic regeneration. The Georgian poet would not, of course, concur in any supposition that the Scandinavian mystic's revelations

and trances were explainable in terms of physiological and psychological factors.

There are grounds for questioning Emerson's insistence on the
unpoetic aspects of Swedenborg's writings, especially after reading
an excerpt from "Solution" (1867). Here over thirty years after his
first essay on Swedenborg he now seems to discover a lyric quality in
the life and spirit of the Swedish theosophist:

> Far in the North, where polar night
> Holds in check the frolic light,
> In trance upborne past mortal goal
> The Swede EMANUEL leads the soul.
> Through snows above, mines underground,
> The inks of EREBUS he found;
> Rehearsed to men the damned wails
> On which the seraph music sails.
> In spirit-worlds he trod alone,
> But walked the earth unmarked, unknown.[44]

While Emerson helped to popularize Swedenborg disciples of the
New Church were spreading his teachings throughout the nation. Its
adherents were small in number but in general zealous and well
educated. Chivers was typical of the select group of Swedenborgians
in the South. A successor to the Georgian, Sidney Lanier (1842-
1881), had some exposure to Swedenborg who in the post bellum
South was a familiar name to intellectuals. An accomplished musician
as well as a poet Lanier read Swedenborg with considerable interest
but did not become a convert to the New Church.[45] Paradoxically he
achieved in his poetry—with better results—the musicality through
harmonious word combinations Chivers sought to attain.

Lanier also recorded accurately the dialect of the black and the
Georgia yeoman, thus sharing another interest with Chivers. Charles
R. Anderson regards the symbolism in "Sunrise" as a result of
Lanier's reading of Swedenborg.[46] Certainly in "Sunrise" he was
trying to penetrate a spiritual or esthetic reality behind the physical
world before his eyes:

> Yea, artist, thou, of whose art yon sea's all news,
> With his inshore greens and manifold mid-sea blues,
> Pearl-glint, shell tint, ancientest perfectest hues
> Even shaming the maidens—lily and rose
> Confess thee, and each mild flame that glows

> In the clarified virginal bosoms of stones that shine,
> It is thine, it is thine.[47]

Still another example of Lanier's fascination with the physical world and the message it sought to communicate to the poet in its own tongue is discernible in "The Symphony." Like Chivers Lanier sensed that nature was speaking to him in a melodious language:

> When Nature from her far-off glen
> Flutes her soft messages to men,
> The flute can say them o'er again;
> Yea, Nature, singing sweet and lone
> Breathes through life's strident polyphone
> The flute-voice in the world of tone.[48]

Lanier's lines and imagery, although composed with a more skillful hand, recall some of Chivers' pleasant poems in *The Lost Pleiad, Eonchs of Ruby,* and *Virginalia*. It is a bit ironic that writers like Emerson and Lanier, attracted to Swedenborg only as a stimulating and original thinker, expressed the theosophist's concepts more succinctly and elegantly than Chivers. Completely absorbed in Swedenborgianism Chivers doubtless fancied his poetry a sublime rendering in verse of the Swedish mystic's profound thoughts expressed in complicated prose. Yet for all his shortcomings Chivers by his unrestrained willingness to experiment did contribute some engaging specimens of verse written to demonstrate the use of words primarily for sonic effects. If not as original as he claimed to be Chivers still merits attention in literary history for his earnest endeavor to apply the theory of correspondences to poetry. Enthusiasm alone unfortunately did not enable Chivers to attain the musicality and haunting refrain of Poe's "The Raven" and "Ulalume." An academic analysis of the theory of correspondences was one matter but applying the theory to poetry required the artistry of a Poe, a quality Chivers lacked.

CHAPTER 3

Nacoochee

I *Summary of Preface and Poem*

Nacoochee; or, the Beautiful Star, With Other Poems which was printed in New York by W. E. Dean in 1837, has a frontispiece that bears a dedication to Chivers' mother who died the following year in 1838. More apt to engage the reader's attention is the preface in which the poet defines poetry in terms symbolic of the mysteries and infinity of the sea:

"Poetry is that crystal river of the soul which runs through all the avenues of life, and after purifying the affections of the heart, empties itself into the Sea of God. Now, he who dives the deepest into that mysterious sea, brings up the greatest number of the shells of truth, and is made richer in the lore of the wisdom of the universe.[1]" Closely united to the Chiversian esthetic, of course, is the Swedenborgian concept of the angel world and divine emanation:

"It is, therefore, evident that the more we investigate the relations that subsist between us and the Creator, the more are our minds expanded, affections matured, and the more are our hopes enlarged in anticipation of the enjoyment of the fellowship of angels, in that other intellectual world, where happiness survives alone, and where we shall assume those beautiful conformities to God, of which we only dream in this. . . .[2]"

Chivers' language becomes somewhat florid as he endeavors to describe the nature of what he considers true poetry. Fragmentary and rough as his metaphors may be, Chivers envisages a new poetry liberated from the traditional restraints of syntax and logic. Words, he seems to be saying, are more than mere sonic emblems of an idea: "Poetry is the soul of his nature, whereby, from communing with the beauties of this earth, he is capable of giving birth to other beings brighter than himself; and of lifting up his spirit to the presence of those things which he shall enjoy in another state; and which he manifests to this through the instrumentality of certain words and sentences melodiously concatenated; and such as correspond with the definite and wise configurations of the mouth in the communication of thought through language.[3]"

"Nacoochee," the title poem covers about thirty pages of the collection. Chivers speaks in the poem of a fabled isle where dwells Nacoochee who yearns for a more perfect state in heaven; up to now she has attained a level just beneath it, the earthly paradise on the island. Two sole survivors of an Indian tribe, Ostenee and his father, Lamorah, discuss the legendary charms of Nacoochee which move the son to begin a long voyage in his canoe to find her. When he finally beholds Nacoochee, he is awestruck by her beauty, but, terrified, Nacoochee calls upon Azrael, the angel of death in Jewish angelology, who comes on his celestial steed to bear her away.

II *Analysis of* Nacoochee

The opening stanza, with its description of the physical beauty of the region, where the story of Nacoochee takes place, is one of many of the poet's word portraits of the Georgian countryside:

> Beyond that wild illimitable waste
> Of unfenced prairie, there are wild
> flowers growing in rich luxuriance,
> ever by the chaste
> And velvet-vested rivers that are
> flowing
> Within the moss-clad suckle valleys
> glowing."[4]

Not quite at ease in handling the descriptive terms, Chivers does impart some musicality to his verse and captures the expansiveness of a wild region of luxuriant beauty. The lush quality in nature perceived here by Chivers has a distinctly Chateaubriandesque flavor. In like manner, Ostenee's father has all the simple majesty of the Indians of Chactas' lineage:

> And there that old chief stood upon the sand,
> Like copper sculptured into majesty!

> For on his dusky brow there sate command,
> And on his lips sublime austerity![5]

Nacoochee undergoes a similar idealization through Chivers' pen and emerges more voluptuous and sexually attractive than the demure maidens of Atala's coterie. If outwardly more alluring than Atala, Nacoochee has inwardly the same religious spirit as Chateaubriand's heroine. Metaphors, somewhat suggestive of the Indian's simple and unadorned imagery, lend a degree of realism to Nacoochee's prayer. Like Atala, she already gives serious thought to death:

> When the mountains, greatly shaken,
> Shall be buried in the sea,
> And my forest home forsaken;
> Lift my spirit up to thee!

Nacoochee goes a step further than Atala in anticipating the joys of heaven. Seraphims watch her from above as she harmonizes her life with celestial precepts:

> There gushed upon her cheeks, beneath her eyes,
> A vigilant sublimity, that seemed
> To those, who gazed upon her with surprise,
> As if they had, despairingly, but dreamed
> Of some Utopian loveliness, they deemed
> Of some celestial sphere, which God had given
> To make creation heaven! Around her beamed
> A living rainbow, softer than the even,
> With two bright, missioned seraphs watching her
>   from heaven!

The reference to angel eloquence and heavenly truths instilled in Nacoochee recalls Swedenborg's observation on the unseen angelic presence in the midst of men and the influx of divine life into the spiritually elite. Nacoochee enjoys this privilege as well as a beauty that causes the poet to interpose himself abruptly into the narrative. Seemingly enraptured with his own creation, Chivers, and not Ostenee, marvels at her sculptural grace. It is the reaction of a civilized white man and not that of a callow savage:

> He looked upon her features with delight
> A chiselled masterpiece almost divine

> The artist, God! She lay along the light
> Of Luna, streaming round her form supine,
> And striving on her loveliness to shine,
> Whose mellow radiance gave unto her eyes
> A languid glory till she seemed to pine
> In her own radiance mingling her surprise
> With that soft innocence which she could not disguise.[8]

After being borne away by Azrael, the angel of death, Nacoochee appears to Ostenee in heavenly splendor, attended by angels and cherubims. She has realized her most lofty ambitions while Ostenee is left with a sense of frustration and unfulfillment:

> And thus enveloped in that mighty flood
> Of everlasting glory, rushed the steed
> To her deliverance! There she stood!
> And who shall recompense that rider for the deed?
> And where was Ostenee? borne like the reed
> That meets the torrent's course he fell like stone!
> But thou, Nacoochee! loved one! thou wert freed
> From this world's sorrow! thou art now alone
> In that bright region round the Eternal's heavenly throne![9]

Since Chivers seems to have intervened once in the narrative to contemplate Nacoochee's beauty, there is little reason not to suppose that Ostenee's regrets are really those of the poet who takes on the air of a frustrated Platonist.[10]

The preface to *Nacoochee* clearly outlines the path Chivers has chosen; his future course will demand a bold effort to create in verse novel effects that strike the eye and ear of the reader. "Nacoochee" is a pleasant poem and a significant step in Chivers' literary development. While inept wording here and there and a weak story line are its patent defects, a reading of "Nacoochee" provides a better understanding of Chivers' development. What the poet produces is a rather strange combination, a Swedenborgian Indian. It is not too difficult to see in Ostenee and Nacoochee the first cousins of Chactas and Atala and to read in Chivers' flowery word portraits an attempt to recapitulate Chateaubriand's panoramic description of the American wilderness. Swedenborgian elements are present in the background. Nacoochee rejects Ostenee in her eagerness to achieve a higher state of grace and thus becomes a more promising candidate for angelic society in heaven. Increasingly God-centered in her thoughts, she spurns the carnal love offered by Ostenee as an obstacle to eternal life for much the same reason Atala refused the love of Chactas. As a true Swedenborgian Nacoochee must gravitate to God for there is no middle ground. The sensual-minded in Swedenborg's system find things divine repugnant and choose instead the world of evil spirits.[11]

Ostenee, usually the villain in Chivers' Indian plays and poems, has a more sympathetic role in "Nacoochee." He is the continental lover in Indian garb. From a Swedenborgian standpoint Ostenee exemplifies the soul that has yet to determine whether his inner tendencies will draw him ultimately to hell—the destination of the lecherous, or to heaven inspired by the example of Nacoochee's purity.

III   *Analysis of Other Poems in the Collection*

The remainder of the collection consists of forty-six poems on a variety of subjects ranging from childhood recollections to those on an Indian theme and ending with the dreary and corny "Malavolti, or the Downfall of the Alamo." The selection immediately following "Nacoochee" is in blank verse, and represents the moment when eternity replaces man's clumsy system for measuring change. In "The Death of Time," the central figure is Christ for whom the stage is set in a manner of reminiscent of the Apocalypse:

> Listen! what mysterious sounds are those
> That roll through heaven? what melodious songs?
> And why that glorious song of ocean, where
> The heavens are mirrored back upon his waste?
> It is the mighty minstrelsy of storms
> Borne on the rustlings of an angel's wings!
> And what is that bright image in the sun?
> An angel fondling with the locks of Christ![12]

Some of Swedenborg's visions of the Last Judgment may have inspired Chivers in the apocalyptic atmosphere created in picturing Christ, conqueror of Death and Hell, in all His glory. Chivers conveys an impression of immensity and the sheer endlessness that will prevail when time is no more. Swedenborg employed the stars and heavens as symbols of divine power and was fond of mentioning horses, dragons, and other animals that communicated to the reader some notion of the overpowering sensations encountered in a mystical experience.[13]

As a poet seeking objects on earth that correspond to higher truths, Chivers selects the sea shell whose echo has a correspondential value when associated with the sublime music heard in heaven:

> Of mighty mountains, whose sky-cleaving heads
> Are crowned with everlasting snows, shall wave
> Their land-tones over ocean, like the shell,
> Whose deep celestial melody shall fly
> To meet the organ of Eternity.
> And roll the waves of thunder into heaven![14]

"The Soaring Swan" is also written in blank verse, a form which enables Chivers to acquit himself competently in a poem of moderate length. Chivers sets the mood from the very first lines, as the physical heights to which the swan soars correspond to the poet's sensation of spiritual elevation:

> Thou art soaring away, beautiful bird!
> Upon thy pinions into distant lands
> Bathing thy downy bosom's loftiest flight
> In welkin zephyrs! Whither art thou borne
> From snowy home through heaven's empyrean depths?
> That seem'st, above my soul's uplifted gaze,
> A snow-fleece newly shorn from Shiloh's lambs,
> And drop half way from heaven! Thou art alone,
> In pearl-tinct azure, pathless, bent for rest,
> As now thy pillowed wings are cleaving heaven![15]

Chivers encourages the bird to persist in its flight and sees perhaps in the swan an image of his own hopes and aspirations which have too often been unrealized. Moreover, Chivers' fascination with the shell image is a foretoken of the theme of *The Eonchs of Ruby* (1851); the correspondential function of the shell has both esthetic and theological implications as a symbol of heavenly music and as an adumbration of the celestial life that awaits man. The poet's growing attraction to Swedenborgianism is in evidence in these lines:

> Beside the tasselled reed-isles, thou shalt hear
> The mellow cadence of the winds, and soothe
> Thy weary soul once more. For there shall flow
> From out the circlings of thy floating form,
> Bathed in the flickering dalliance of the gems

> Of thy sun-cinctured dimples, like the pearl
> Of ocean set in beryl by the deep
> A shell-toned music whose deep sound shall be
> As soft as that sweet sigh of angels when
> They whisper to the soul celestial peace.[16]

The possible influence of Coleridge has been discerned in "The Soaring Swan," and J. A. Harrison feels the poem had some effect on Rossetti.[17] PreSymbolistic tendencies in Chivers are manifest in his effort to evoke a response from the reader; colors and sounds to stimulate the imagination are softly suggested, and much is left to the individual in the formation of his particular impressions.

"Man's Life," restates Chivers' trust in God reinforced with scriptural references. The reader senses at times a desire on Chivers' part to play the Baptist preacher,[18] especially when the poem seems to echo with hymn singing and gospel preaching:

> His life is like the mountain stream
>   That wends along through hillcocks steep,
> That wider grows while others teem,
>   Till lost in ocean's briny deep.
> And thus man's life renews, decays
>   Through time's eventful changes free
> Though many shoals obstruct his ways,
>   And ends like rivers meet the sea.[19]

"Ode to the Mississippi" possesses provincial warmth and honesty; he expresses his admiration of the "Father of Waters" in terms that do credit to his Southern heritage. In view of Chivers' fondness for Chateaubriand, there is cause to speculate on the extent to which the French writer sharpened his awareness of the majesty of the Mississippi. A Northern writer, Harriet Beecher Stowe, in the midst of *Uncle Tom's Cabin*, also recalled how Chateaubriand had portrayed the magnificence of the mighty river.[20]

> Thou "Father of Waters!" thou million in one!
> Oh! speak from the North where thy travels begun,
> And tell me the first with thyself to unite,
> Who walked down the valley like lovers at night,
> Till thou, with thy freedom majestic and deep,
> Bestrode like an emperor walking in sleep.[21]

The emotions engendered by viewing the Mississippi may date from Chivers' period of exile and describe his deeply felt impressions of that painful time. "To My Mother," which has the subtitle "Written Beyond the Mountains," suggests that Chivers wandered many miles west of Saint Louis into the then wilderness.[22]

The mood and quality of the poems in *Nacoochee* vary greatly. After some maudlin lines of graveyard poetry "Stanzas for Music" betrays a wistful longing for bygone days and a somber meditation on the meaning of time. Like many Romantics, Chivers is disturbed by the impermanence he senses about him, the constant state of flux that leads nowhere:

> We feel that existence belongs to the past,
> And cling unto hopes that remain;
> And mend every harp-string, though breaking as fast,
> But never shall strike them again!
> And thus, only left with affection, forlorn,
> We sigh all alone like the dove
> That hastens away from her nest but to mourn,
> And die for the loss of her love![23]

The remaining poems in the volume are of little consequence. *Malavolti*, a narrative poem about the Alamo, abounds in such ridiculous clichés that its plot is best left unmentioned.

Chivers, at this juncture, was not just another Romantic poet on the American scene worthy of only passing mention. The Georgian was beginning to grasp some of the full significance of the use of words, divorced from their traditional conceptual function, to designate inner states of the soul and to convey sensory impressions. This feature constitutes the most meaningful aspect of *Nacoochee*.

CHAPTER 4

The Lost Pleiad

I *Background of Publication*

The Lost Pleiad, and Other Poems was printed by Edward O. Jenkins in New York in 1845. As usual Chivers paid the bill. He felt more than amply compensated when Poe gave a high rating to many poems in *The Lost Pleiad* and scored the canons of so-called good taste applied to this publication by many overly pedantic critics in the East. To Poe, a bright and original outlook was necessary to appreciate Chivers' talent: "The poems of Dr. Chivers abound in what must undoubtedly be considered as gross demerit, if we admit the prevalent canons of criticism. But it may safely be maintained that these prevalent canons have, in no great part, no surer foundation than arrant conventionality. Be these things as they may, we have no hesitation in saying that we consider many of the pieces in the volume before us as possessing merit of a very lofty if not of the very loftiest. order."[1] William Gilmore Simms also complimented Chivers on his originality but complained about the work's unnatural gloom and melancholy. As for the title, Simms indicated its previous use by Letitia E. Landon,[2] but ample precedent existed for the popularity of "Lost Pleiad" as a poetic theme since Simms had himself copied it. To Chivers' credit, it should be noted that had he previously utilized the "Lost Pleiad" as a symbol in *The Path of Sorrow* and in *Nacoochee*. After some initial success, there was a rapid decline in the sales of *The Lost Pleiad*, but Chivers at least had the benefit of enjoying for a fleeting moment some degree of recognition.

II *Analysis*

Edward Young's *Night Thoughts* provided mottoes for many of Chivers' poems most of which are rather short. The longest, the title

46

poem, consists of over eight hundred lines on the death of the poet's little daughter, Allegra Florence. Most of the poems in *The Lost Pleiad* are elegies about members and friends of the Chivers' family as well as historical figures ranging from Shakespeare to Washington. The "Prefatory Apologue," dated July 18, 1845, furnishes some insight into Chivers' mystical frame of mind when composing *The Lost Pleiad,* for he had a Swedenborgian sense of the immediacy of the spirit world:

A SHEPHERD was mourning over the death of his favorite child, and, in the passionate and rebellious feeling of his heart, was bitterly complaining that what he loved most tenderly, and was, in itself, most lovely, had been taken away from him. Suddenly, a STRANGER, of grave and venerable appearance, stóod before him, and beckoned him forth into the field. It was night, and not a word was spoken till they arrived at the field, when the STRANGER thus addressed him: "When you select one of these lambs from the flock, you choose the best and most beautiful among them. Why should you murmur because I, the GOOD SHEPHERD of the sheep, have selected from those which you have nourished for me, the one most fitted for my Eternal Fold?" The MYSTERIOUS STRANGER was seen no more, and the father's heart was comforted.[3]

This preface also sets the mood for the title poem in which a grief stricken Chivers asks God to provide an explanation for the sudden death of an innocent child. His depiction of the dying girl is one of the few occasions on which he uses his medical background to detail the symptoms of typhoid fever; the realism of Chiver's description brings power and conviction to the poem:

> And then, with more than mortal dread
> I laid my hand upon her head!
> It was as clammy cold with sweat,
> As roseleaves in the frost-dew wet!
> I wiped away the death-cold dew
> Her once soft pearly nails were blue!
> The cramp was in her hands and feet!
> Her breath, that once was more than sweet
> Than Jessamines when first in bloom
> Smelt like the cold earth of the tomb!
> For, oh! the agonizing pain
> Had palsied her young tender brain,
> Till were the pupils of her eyes
> Dilated twice their natural size!

> The pearly alae of her nose,
> Like frost-bit petals of the rose,
> Were both contracted, cold and thin;
> And her blue eyes had both sunk in!
> And her soft, heart-enfolding breast
> Kept panting with that heart's unrest!
> For, as her feeble breath grew thick,
> Her thread-like pulse became more quick!
> And then her pale, cold lips I kist,
> And laid my hand upon her wrist!
> Her pulse had almost ceased to beat!
> And then I felt her icy feet!

The memory of his daughter's fever racked body still cannot remove the vision of celestial life as Chivers envisages her state in heaven clothed in her spiritual body after having cast aside the outer shell of the material body:

> So does the soul cast off its form
> Even as the chrysalis the worm
> And rise up from its mortal night,
> A spiritual body, clothed in light,
> As different from its body here,
> As Heaven is from this sinful sphere.[5]

Chivers' concept of the afterlife is modeled on Swedenborgian lines. Hence he depicts heaven, by tradition an immaterial realm, in decidedly material terms. The body of the deceased is glorified and transfused with light, a visual phenomenon dwelt upon by Swedenborg when relating visits to the spirit world. Mention of the spiritual body is in keeping with the notion of correspondences; a spiritual reality is a counterpart to a material one. His daughter is now ready to enter angelic society since Swedenborg teaches that all angels were once men on earth.

The sorrow of a bereaved father is normal but Chivers' attachment to his mother, while to some degree understandable, becomes excessive in its manifestations. Regression, a longing for childhood and its less complicated demands and situations, was a general symptom of Romantic melancholia. Presentday Freudians would have a fruitful source of psychoanalytical studies in passages like the following from "To My Mother in Heaven":

> I FEEL an ardent longing for thy love,
> A yearning for that SPIRIT-LAND above!
> A wounded spirit is the one to feel,
> By suffering, what it is to value weal!
> I long to lay me in my resting-place,
> And cradle me again in thy embrace;
> And stay my wounded spirit on thy breast
> The only one that ever gave me rest![6]

The straightforwardness of the first two poems, "The Lost Pleiad" and "To My Mother in Heaven," compensates in some measure for the maudlin commonplaces in "The Orphan's Prayer," "The Mother's Lament on the Death of Her Child," and similar pieces. Poe overlooked Chivers' lacklustre poems and emphasized those whose rhythm and harmony he naturally found more appealing such as "The Wife's Lament for Her Husband Lost at Sea." Chivers' use of the refrain provides a mournful echo to lines whose cadence subtlely captures the action of the sea's waves:

> I hear thy spirit calling unto me
> From out the Deep,
> Like lost Archytas from Venetia's Sea,
> While here I weep!
> Saying, Come, strew my body with the sand
> And bury me upon the land, the land!
> Oh! never, never more! no, never more!
> Lost in the Deep,
> While thy sweet beauty visit this dark shore,
> While I here weep!
> For thou art gone forever more from me,
> Sweet Mariner! lost murdered by the Sea![7]

The above lines bear a faint resemblance to "Oceano Nox" in which Victor Hugo had similar reflections on sailors lost at sea. Hugo conveyed through the undulating cadence of his lines an impression of the incessant rolling of ocean waves on the shores, a constant reminder that the sea claimed many victims. Chivers achieves through repetition of key words a somewhat similar effect; the result in the Georgian's poetry is a gentle ripple of the waves compared to the impression created by Hugo. In the latter the lines of "Oceano Nox" capture the full effect of mighty waves lashing the shore.

Like the preceding poem, "To Allegra Florence in Heaven"[8] with its a-a-a-b rhyme scheme is also of interest; avoiding the pitfalls of sing-songishness, Chivers demonstrates his sense of rhythm and harmony. When read aloud, the auditory aspect of the lines over-shadows their literal meaning. The simultaneous sensation of the angels' descent and the ascent of Allegra's soul to join them produces a mixed feeling of joy and sorrow:

> Holy angels now are bending
> To receive thy soul ascending
> Up to Heaven to joys unending,
>   And to bliss which is divine;
> While thy pale, cold form is fading
> Under death's dark wings now shading
> Thee with gloom which is pervading
> This poor, broken heart of mine.[9]

In the same poem is the notorious simile of the egg that was ridiculed even by critics usually sympathetic to Chivers:

> As an egg, when broken, never
> Can be mended, but must ever
> Be the same crushed egg forever
> So shall this dark heart of mine!
> Which, though broken, is still breaking
> And shall never more cease aching
> For the sleep which has no waking
> For the sleep which now is thine![10]

An irresistible temptation to laugh overcomes the reader at the notion of Chivers' taking seriously a well-known nursery rhyme and likening his own sense of personal loss to the fate of Humpty-Dumpty. Still a more serious interpretation is conceivable given Chivers' consistent adherence to Swedenborg. To the sober Swedish mystic, the egg was a prefectly respectable symbol which he utilized in the *Arcana Coelestia* to explain how man gradually evolved in attaining wisdom and maturity; man was, in this sense, being continuously reborn.[11] For Chivers, the egg may have connoted a new stage of sorrow felt for the first time when his daughter died.

Chivers spent his time more profitably when composing poems like the one dedicated to Shelley. Watts has noted that Shelley's most important contribution to Chivers' development was to refine and curb the Georgian's unrestrained and aimless impulses.[12] The desire to identify himself with Shelley's quest for truth and beauty was a temptation Chivers found difficult to resist:

> Thou didst desire the unadulterate truth,
> As one who seeks what may be found, if sought
> The first love of his heart in earliest youth
> Though not amid the realms of mortal thought
> And soaring far beyond all things, didst bring
> Back unto Man the truths which Angels sing.[13]

Some of Shelley's capacity for elevating the readers' spirits is caught by Chivers in "The Soul's Destiny" which Poe judged one of the volume's better selections. Unable to accept death as the terminus of human destiny, Chivers envisions eternal life and, for a fleeting second, shares Shelley's vision of the celestial verities sought by the artist:

> Say! are we doomed to wander here,
> The ghosts of what we were
> Watching above each sepulchre
> The form that moulders there?
> Or, shall we sleep beneath the sod,
> When this dark life shall cease?
> Or, shall we soar away to God,
> And dwell with Him in peace?[14]

"Lament on the Death of My Mother" is not a title that would suggest a poem later linked to the Poe-Chivers controversy and bitter charges of plagiarism, but the refrain and the series of statements in the negative furnish more than a faint hint of a similarity in structure. "The Raven" and Chivers' poem to his mother are both elegies, but Poe's is in dialogue form. Chivers' meditation on death is stated in more universal terms with a grace and movement that do not suffer notably from any comparison with the haunting beauty of "The Raven."

> Not while the children of the Spring shall smile,
>   And strew my path with flowers of every hue
> Cooling the fever of my heart the while,
>   With goblets brimful of nectarian dew;
> Not while the younglings of her lap shall shine,

> Wilt thou return to this dark home of mine
>   No, never more!
> Not till the orange bowers that wooed us long,
>   Where Love first haunted me in heavenly dreams
> Where Sorrow voiced itself away in song
>   Shall pass away, with all our crystal streams;
> Shall such sad partings, on life's barren shore,
> Be changed for meetings which shall part no more
>   No, never more![15]

In another poem on the theme of death Chivers depicts quite effectively a dream in which the spirit of his daughter returns to visit him. At home in describing apparitions and trance-like states, similar to those that affected Swedenborg, Chivers vividly describes an eerie experience in "The Heavenly Vision:"

> Long had we parted long had she been dead
>   When late, one night, when all had gone to rest,
> Her spirit stood before me near my bed
>   She came from Heaven to tell me she was blest.
> As some fond Dove unto her own mate sings,
>   So sang she unto me, in my unrest,
> (Who lay beneath the shadow of her wings
>   Of Heaven, wherein she told me she was blest.[17]

Chivers moves easily from reality to the area of oneiroscopy when depicting dreams. Readily susceptible to autosuggestion and hallucinations, the poet records such experiences with fidelity and shifts easily from consciousness to the dream state.

There is no available evidence that Chivers was addicted to drugs, although the ascertainment of addiction in the nineteenth century would have been more difficult than it is today. Opium was then used in several forms of medication and often many persons unknowingly became addicted to the drug during childhood. Although Chivers was a doctor he did not practice his profession long enough to recognize more subtle clinical symptoms even in himself. Knowledge of the true nature of opium was then relatively unsophisticated. The possible effect of opium on Chivers' mind could account for his insistence on the reality of his visions, a conviction strengthened by his belief in Swedenborg's revelations. While the notion of a drug related factor to explain Chivers' dreams may at first seem far-fetched, it is not beyond the realm of reasonable conjecture when the cases of

Coleridge and DeQuincey are recalled. Awareness of narcotics and their effects, though common knowledge today, was not widespread in the nineteenth century.

Evidence of drug addiction is not required to explain the unevenness of inspiration in the moody Chivers. When reading *The Lost Pleiad*, the reader patiently endures the mediocrity of poems like "My Soul's Jewel" and "The Salutation" to come upon a just reward for his efforts. After reading "Sonnet To Isa Sleeping," Poe's favorable response to the finesse and harmony of this sonnet is quite comprehensible:

> As graceful as the Babylonian willow
> Bending, at noontide, over some clear stream
> In Palestine, in beauty did she seem
> Upon the cygnet-down of her soft pillow;
> And now her breast heaved like some gentle billow
> Swayed by the presence of the full round moon
> Voluptuous as the summer South at noon
> Her cheeks as rosy as the radiant dawn
> When heaven is cloudless! When she breathed, the air
> Around was perfume! Timid as the fawn,
> And meeker than the dove, her soft words were
> Like gentle music heard at night, when all
> Around is still until the soul of care
> Was soothed, as noontide by some waterfall.[18]

The sensuousness of Chivers' word portrait and effortless use of clear and direct terms to convey sensory impressions demonstrate that his forte lay in poems of medium length. His longer compositions are often redeemed in part by isolated passages even though the overall merit of the poem may be negligible. In "Sonnet to Isa Sleeping," Chivers' provincialism is perceptible. While Isa might be termed a Babylonian belle, Chivers is obviously describing a Southern beauty reclining by a stream in Georgia.

An artless externalization of his inner feelings was quite characteristic of Chivers; this facet of his personality is easily seen in "The Poet's Love of Fame." Hypersensitive to all criticism of his poems, Chivers tells readers that the lasting fame of a writer after death is commendable but a little recognition in this life too has its compensations:

> But, though, within our mortal, we can see
> Nothing which looks immortal to our sight;

> Behind that veil there is what makes us be,
>   And without which we soon would be all night.
> And as Man's natural body lives on earth,
>   With earthly things seen with our natural eyes
> Our spiritual bodies shall, when we go forth
>   Be seen by spiritual ones, where nothing
> Then, we shall see all things as they are
>   On earth, with eyes no mortal sun can
> And be in Heaven as we have ever been,
>   Like man, though a subject not to death
> And if we carry with us all we have
>   Of knowledge here below, or happiness;
> The more we have of each, this side the grave
>   The richer will we be in heavenly bliss.[19]

Spiritual eyes replace the corporeal ones man uses on earth, and life in the celestial sphere continues as it did in material existence as once more Swedenborg is drawn upon to strengthen belief in eternal life. The date affixed to "The Poet's Love of Fame," April 1, 1841, offers proof that at the start of the 1840's Chivers was a confirmed Swedenborgian.

In "Spring," Chivers beholds a mystical significance in that bright season. The "crystal river" of which he speaks may allude to the primitive revelations expounded by Jakob Behmen, the German mystic and theologian, and the sun depicted by Chivers might well refer to the spiritual sun described in *Arcana Coelestia*.[20] The Georgian probably was at least acquainted with Behmist commonplaces through his reading of Swedenborgian and spiritualist publications:

> Thou art the fountain whence the crystal river
>   Of the warm year, from month to month, do run,
> Whose waves are days, which, flower-gemmed
>   flows forever
> Out of the Golden Mountain of the Sun.[21]

One form for which Chivers had a knack was the ballad. "Awake from Thy Slumbers" has a gentle, lilting movement that reminds the reader of Stephen Foster. Chivers' love of the countryside and birds, in particular, imparts a certain sprightliness to the sentiments expressed:

> Awake from thy slumbers! the wild birds are tuning
> Their voices to greet thee so loud in the brake,
> While the roebucks are watching the swans
>   that are pruning
> Their white silver wings on the glass of the lake.[22]

Love of nature was a most acceptable Romantic convention and the necessary trademark of a poet of that era. Another such convention that Chivers occasionally felt obliged to observe was the morbid brooding on death provided in "The Dying Poet," one of several versions he wrote:

> My young years' youngest flowers that grew,
>   And garlanded my brow,
> Are slain beneath the heavy dew,
>   And all are withered now![23]

Byron, Keats, and Shelley are likely sources for such sentiments, but another that should not be disregarded is Lamartine who was widely read and admired in both the North and South during the first half of the nineteenth century. Among the selections from the French poet's *Méditations* most commonly translated in American magazines was *Le poète mourant.* Chivers was familiar with Lamartine's work and probably read translations of *Le poète mourant.* Although evidence indicates that his knowledge of French was limited, in view of his fondness for Chateaubriand, he might well have been attracted to another French Romantic.[24]

Amidst a seemingly endless succession of elegies that sound more like funeral dirges, Chivers provides a welcome surprise by a happy, little poem on Allegra Florence's birth:

> Thou art prophetic of what is to be
>   A Heaven on earth, which tells of Heaven above
> Wherein all that my soul has longed to see,
>   Is seen revealed to me in heavenly love.[25]

The reference to a promise of "Heaven on earth" links Chivers to the Utopian movements and communities being established in the United States and patterned after the Associationist principles of Charles Fourier to whom on one occasion he dedicated a poem. Chivers dreamed of realizing on earth the ideal celestial society described by Swedenborg. Included in this earthly paradise would undoubtedly be many a fair maid if Chivers' frequent references to feminine pulchritude are any indication.

The poet's preferences are difficult to judge by current standards. A poem dedicated to a composer somewhat neglected today, Carl Maria Von Weber, bears witness to the tastes of another era. Readers at the time appreciated what Chivers was saying in praise of Weber. An ardent music lover who often attended operas and concerts when up North, Chivers illustrates in "On Hearing Von Weber's Last Waltz" the emotions felt when listening to a favorite composer:

> For it tells of the rapture, the gladness, the love
>   Of the Seraph-winged soul, when the body is dying
> When the windows of Heaven are opened above
>   To receive it, while upward to Paradise flying;
> And it tells here on earth of the bliss, the delight
>   In the language of Angels, that Angels are feeling,
> And reveals to the soul, what the soul, in its flight
>   Up to Heaven, of that Heaven to the world is revealing;
> Until weary of earth, unto my soul seems given
>   The wings of an Angel to bear me to Heaven. [26]

Chivers cannot resist the urge to inject a Swedenborgian note, particularly in the matter of angels and angelic language. The music of Von Weber invokes a vision of heaven in which Chivers anticipates Baudelaire and the French Symbolists in recording his impressions of a specific musical composition. The simple device of repeating key words, used in the poem to Weber, is employed with greater effect in "The Mother's Lament on the Death of Her Child":

> The funeral bell keeps tolling, keeps tolling,
>   Keeps tolling for the dead;
> Whose azure round goes rolling, goes rolling,
>   Like waters, o'er my head! [27]

Another point in the Poe-Chivers controversy is evident in the similarity of the Georgian's lines to "The Bells." *The Lost Pleiad* was the volume from which, Chivers insisted, Poe acquired not a few ideas about imagery and meter.

There are also sensual reflections in *The Lost Pleiad* that serve as a reminder that Chivers, sincere as his confessions of belief might be, was not a monk. "Anacreontique" portrays something more than just innocent passion:

> My hand would steal, like heavenly Hope
>   To Adam from the Garden driven,
> With trembling, down they bosom's slope,
>   As he to enter his lost Heavens. [28]

Less passionate, however, are the sentiments addressed to another imaginary lass whose charms are compared to various blossoms. "To Jesse" is of interest as a reflection of Chivers' concern with olfactory sensations and of his familiarity with the flora of the South:

> The ROSE is called the Queen of all the Flowers
>   More radiant, but of odor less divine;
> The rich MAGNOLIA, though it scent the bowers
>   Afar, is far less sweet than JESSAMINE!
> The PEACH-TREE blossom is of "tender smell"
>   So is the saintly APPLE-BLOOM divine;
> But never TUBEROSE, from Indian dell,
>   Could be compared with thee, my JESSAMINE! [29]

A more subtle appeal to the senses appears in "The Cherished Flower" in which Chivers centers on one flower, a rose, whose fragrance provides a point of departure for reminiscing. In this poem, where Chivers reinvigorates a timeworn cliché, he also presents one of his more pleasing poetic moods, applies a light touch, and injects an ingratiatingly wistful note:

> Amid the green things of my life's young spring,
>   One ROSE there was which bloomed serenely bright,
> From whose sweet leaves the zephyrs used to bring
>   Odors which wafted me to pure delight.
> I treasured every breath of air that came
>   To waft its cherished redolence away
> Because, through every change, it was the same
>   More beautiful by night than by the day. [30]

III *Summary of* The Lost Pleiad

The presence of unmistakably Swedenborgian themes in *The Lost Pleiad* establishes that by the 1840's Chivers was a supporter of the theology of the New Church. A heaven realized in human terms, the light phenomena beheld in visions, the notion of correspondences, and the spiritual sun are commonplaces drawn from Swedenborg to which Chivers refers in his poems. A zealot who read with conviction the mystical experiences of Swedenborg, he acquired a surprising aptitude to describe trance-like states as well as the objects and the phenomena perceived in dreams.

Religion was deeply personal to Chivers who could not keep from expressing the hopes, sorrows, and frustrations affecting his own life. Chivers' attachment to his mother at times has almost Freudian implications despite the fact that filial love, like regression, is a fairly common Romantic tendency.

Chivers in many ways merits the label of Romantic. The melancholy of a Young or a Byron he assumes quite easily. The oppressed minorities of countries subjected to tyranny receive his sympathy, and he has an eager eye for feminine beauty. On the social plane he alludes to a Utopian society. His love of nature, while a Romantic convention, is the most genuine aspect of Chivers' Romanticism and a reflection of his fondness of the Georgian countryside. Equally sincere is his admiration of Washington even though the adulation tends to become a bit Victor Hugo-ish.

On the esthetic side, Chivers displays finesse in handling imagery and meter. The refrain in his hands is at times utilized to good effect. In sharing Shelley's vision of beauty, Chivers is not satisfied to merely emulate the great English poet. Stimulated by Swedenborg's statement about correspondences, he seeks material images that reflect celestial truths. In this process, he sees the interrelation of music and poetry, a perception that marks one of the more advanced features of *The Lost Pleiad*.

IV   Search After Truth

Search After Truth; or, A New Revelation of the Psycho-Physiological Nature of Man was published in New York by Cobb and Yallalee in 1848. Poe probably read a rough draft of *Search After Truth* under the title *Luciferian Revelation*, but the manuscript was never published as Chivers had requested.[31] Little guess work was needed to ascertain that *Search After Truth* was a repetition in greater detail of arguments probably used by Chivers to convert Poe. In the work Chivers assigns himself the role of the Seer and nicknames Poe, "Politian," after the latter's drama.[32]

Much of the treatise consists of lengthy discourses by the Seer on religion, philosophy, and Swedenborgianism in reply to leading questions from Politian. Of the ancient philosophers, Plato is designated by the Seer as the foremost defender of man's spiritual nature. The sensism of John Locke receives treatment as a prime example of a dangerously materialistic school of thought. With proof of the existence of the soul once incontrovertibly established to the Seer's satisfaction, Politian is subjected to a detailed exposition of Swedenborg's teaching on man's state in paradise, the organization of angelic society, and the theory of correspondences. The Seer also endeavors to show that all religions throughout the ages have insisted on the immortality of the soul.

Most of Chivers' quasimetaphysical speculations are delivered in a pedestrian manner, and only on occasion is there any indication that poetry is his primary concern. One passage, decidedly theosophic in tone, speaks of the person endowed with a superior perception of divine mysteries and of the esthetic aspect of creation: "It is only by living in harmony with all things, that Man can understand the expression of God's Beautiful in the world. It is only by having his eyes couched that he can look, as the High Priest of Nature, from the star-lighted Sanctuary of this world into the Angel-lighted Arcana of Heaven. . . ."[33]

From Swedenborg and Jakob Behmen Chivers may have obtained the reference to man as the "High Priest of Nature"; to them the priesthood, somewhat like the angelic state, signified the level of perfection man enjoyed before the Fall. "We shall lead a Holy Priestly Life" when spiritually regenerated, predicted Behmen, who relates how Adam originally lost the kingly priesthood, so that natural man by his own power and virtue could no longer offer sacrifice to God.[34] Similarly, Swedenborg likened celestial men, those who had attained a high state of spirituality, to the priesthood of Jehovah. In his explanation of the symbolic meaning of terms, Swedenborg stated that priests were those in a state of goodness and love of the Lord.[35]

The concept of man as a priest, or as one destined to play a sacerdotal role, was already a commonplace with the early European Romantics. Novalis (Freiherr von Hardenberg) in *Blossom Dust* (*Blütenstaub*), evidently enlarged on a concept derived from Behmen and Swedenborg in identifying the poet with persons who, in primitive times, occupied privileged positions. "Bards and priests were one and the same in the beginning. Only later ages have sundered them. The true poet is always a priest, just as the true priest

has always remained a poet."[36] William Blake also believed that the
ancient poets constituted a priesthood in their singing of divine
praises, a concept he most likely acquired directly or indirectly from
Behmen and Swedenborg.[37]

French Romantics also entertained a high estimate of the poet's
hieratic function; strongly influenced as some of them were by the
illuminists of the eighteenth century, they most likely read the
description by one well-known Theosophist in France, Louis-Claude
de Saint-Martin, of man's calling to be "le Prêtre de l'Éternel dans
l'Univers."[38]

Chivers followed a precedent well established among European
Romantics with theosophic leanings when he attributed sacerdotal
powers to those possessing special insights into the divine plan. In
fact, an adequate understanding of *Search After Truth* is difficult
unless the teachings of Swedenborg are taken into consideration. The
Seer who leads the discussion derives his title very likely from the fact
that Swedenborg was termed a seer by admiring disciples. The
format brings to mind Jakob Behmen's "A Dialogue Between A
Scholar and His Master Concerning the Supersensual Life" in which
the Master says that, when the visible world is gone, there shall
remain only the "Chrystalline Nature and Form" of man since human
beings will then be like the spiritual world that replaces the old
sensory order.[39] Since Swedenborg was influenced by Behmen, any
disciple of the Swedish mystic would have little compunction in
consulting the German Theosophist. George Bush, Swedenborgian
apologist and theologian to whom Chivers gave a copy of *Search After
Truth*, might well have encouraged the Georgian writer to read
Behmen for Bush corresponded rather frequently with Chivers. The
description of the spiritual essence of creation, "Chrystalline Nature
and Form" was probably derived from Behmen by Chivers and used
to symbolize the arcana hidden from ordinary mortals. Only the poet
could penetrate these truths as one specially ordained by God to be a
priest in the theosophic sense of the word. This then is the message of
Search After Truth that primarily concerns the student of Chivers'
poetry. The remainder of the treatise is only of passing interest as a
specimen of Chivers' bombastic utterances on a wide range of
subjects: Platonism, philology, Aristotle, and the Bible to mention a
few.

CHAPTER 5

Eonchs of Ruby

I *Chivers' Comments in Preface*

CHIVERS reimbursed Spalding and Shepard of New York for publishing *Eonchs of Ruby, A Gift of Love* in 1851. A definition of the work's odd title was later provided by the poet in the *Georgia Citizen*: "The Word *Eonch* is the same as *Concha Marina—Shell of the Sea. Eonch* is used instead of *Concha*, merely for its euphony. It is the same as the Kaur Gaur of the Hebrews. Ruby signifies, in the language of correspondence, *Divine Love.* The word *Eonch* is used, as a title, by metonymy, for *Songs.* The meaning of the title is, therefore, apparent namely, *Songs of Divine Love.* The clouds, I hope, are now dispelled; and the mystery, I presume, evaporates. I hope the day will continue clear."[1]

The subtitle indicates Chivers' desire to capitalize on the current fetish for gift books; but he was also keeping pace with another contemporary trend by using an obscure title that required an occultist explanation. Mediums and Spiritualists, very much in vogue, used to utter strange sounds, purportedly the speech of the spirit world. Swedenborgians were studying the description of angelic language which, according to *Heaven and Hell*, consisted only of vowel sounds. Chivers' indebtedness to Swedenborg is disclosed in his definition of "Ruby" as "Divine Love" in the "language of Correspondence." To the Swedish mystic precious stones were emblems of supernatural truths.[2]

About half of the forty poems in *Eonchs of Ruby* had previously appeared in magazines; and since Chivers' name was fairly well-known by 1851, the work at first drew the attention of readers and critics. Some of the latter had favorable comments, but there were also enough caustic remarks to irk Chivers. Poems with a Poesque flavor were to set off an argument over the extent to which the Georgian had plagiarized Poe.

II   *Analysis of* Eonchs of Ruby

Since the first poem "The Vigil of Aiden" is a homage to Poe, any borrowing in this instance could be condoned for Chivers was paying tribute to his colleague. The opening lines have a cadence and melody that recall Poe's best lyrics:

> In the Rosy Bowers of Aiden,
> With her ruby-lips love-laden,
> Dwelt the mild, the modest Maiden
>   Whom POLITIAN called LENORE.
> As the Churches, with their whiteness
> Clothe the earth, with her uprightness
> Clothed she now his soul with brightness,
>   Breathing out her heart's love-lore;[3]

Politian, none other than Poe in a thinly veiled disguise, mourns the impending loss of Lenore. The mood and rhythm of "The Raven" are invoked by Chivers to picture the sorrowful Politian inquiring of his beloved whether their two souls will meet again. Chivers' imitation of Poe here is quite acceptable:

> "Are we not to meet, dear Maiden!
> In the Rosy Bowers of Aiden,
> As we did in Days of Yore?"
> And the voice of that sweet Maiden,
> From the Jasper Groves of Aiden
> With her lily-lips love-laden,
> Answered, "Yes! forever more!"[4]

If the structure of "The Vigil in Aiden" is Poesque, the theology is definitely Chiversian. Poe was, on the whole, indifferent to religion, unlike Chivers who eagerly depicts his ubiquitous band of angels waiting to whisk some fortunate soul off to heaven; in this instance, Lenore is the lucky one. A carryover from Chivers' Baptist days was belief in the machinations of the devil; hence, true to form, Lucifer soon appears to test the sincerity of Politian's fidelity to Lenore:

> Then, beside the silent river,
> Where he wandered still forever,
> By her lonely grave that ever
>   Seemed to Heaven the only door—
> Through the amethystine morning

> Came foul Lucifer returning
> Up from Hell, where he was burning—
> This Elysian chant to pour—[5]

Lucifer attempts various ruses to weaken Politian, but none succeed. The finale has the spirit of Lenore return to Politian to announce his salvation. Here Chivers gives his own version of the Faust legend:

> "Are we not to meet, dear Maiden!
> In the Heavenly Bowers of Aiden,
> On the Asphodelian shore?"
> And that glorified sweet Maiden,
> From the Heavenly Bowers of Aiden,
> With her lily-lips love-laden,
>   Answered, "Yes! FOREVER MORE!"
> And the God-built Towers of Aiden
> Echoed, "Yes! forever more!"[6]

Politian, encouraged by Lenore's revelation, resists the blandishments of Lucifer with a Christian steadfastness that would be foreign to Poe. "The Vigil of Aiden" ends with Politian and Lenore, attended by Chiversian angels, ascending to heaven in a chariot.

The second poem in the volume, "The Mighty Dead," is another lengthy elegy. Among the famous figures eulogized by Chivers in "The Mighty Dead" is William Henry Harrison (1773-1841)—for whom he has a few Swedenborgian words of wisdom about the happy destiny of the spiritual body:

> All that could die is dead!
> Thy body is as senseless as the grave!
>   But thy undying Soul to Heaven hast fled—
> A spiritual body—Christ alone could save!
>   A perfect being, without parts—one whole—
> Is now the nature of thy God-made soul.[7]

The association of Swedenborg with American liberty is implied by Chivers who assigns to Harrison a hieratic role in leading Americans to a New Jerusalem, the Swedish mystic's term for a revitalized spiritual order.[8]

In the profusion of oratorical passages in "The Mighty Dead," there is an occasional one where Chivers speaks more calmly—as when honoring the memory of Edward Young. The lightning and thunder in the heavens recede and Chivers utilizes tender and sensuous images to recreate the climate of Young's lugubrious lines:

> Like that Sorrowful Tree,
> Whose blossoms only flourish in the night,
>   Making the silence fragrant with its sea
> Of odor—clouding darkness with the light
>   Of moonlit incense—thou didst Heaven divine
> With Music's love-unfolded Eglantine.[9]

When praising Shelley in "The Mighty Dead" Chivers pauses momentarily in his oratorial flights of fancy to render one stanza that does justice to both himself and the English poet:

> Like that sweet Bird of Night,
> Startling the ebon silence from repose,
>   Until the stars appear to burn more bright
> From its excessive gush of song, which flows
>   Like some impetuous river to the sea—
> So thou did'st flood the world with melody.[10]

Among the figures praised in "The Mighty Dead," some remain well-known today; others are given little or no attention. This contrast becomes apparent when comparing Washington, Milton, and Shakespeare, for example, to Felicia Hemans, Edward Young, and Marco Botzaris.

The third poem, "Avalon," also an elegy of considerable length, concerns the death of his oldest son, Eugene Percy. Chivers' love of nature in springtime blends with an unaffected expression of grief and a desperate plea to God to assuage his sorrow:

> My little Lambs are scattered now abroad
> In Death's dark Valley, where they bleat unheard!
> Dear Shepherd! give their Shepherd his reward
>   Where they are lying
>   Beside the beautiful undying
> In the Valley of the pausing of the Moon,
> With AVALON! my son! my son![11]

In the above stanza can be observed those facets of Chivers' thinking that deeply influence his religious and esthetic outlook.

Faith in Christ justifies in the poet's mind hope for reunion in heaven. Earnest and profound emotions furnish Chivers what he considers some of the best and most human themes to be expressed in poetry. Although the poet finds it difficult to reconcile these brutal facts with his faith, what seems a sign of divine anger, the loss of his children, can be explained only if he finds comfort in his poetry:

> Can less than bringing back the early dead,
>   Restore my soul?
> No! this alone can make my Heavenly bread—
> Christ's Bread of Life brought down from Heaven, instead
> Of this sad Song, on which my soul has fed,
>   Where thou art lying
>   Beside the beautiful undying
> In the Valley of the pausing of the Moon,
> Oh! AVALON! my son! my son! [12]

The hymnal quality of "Avalon" and the directness achieved by its refrains make the lines ring true. Awkwardness in some of the rhymes does not detract from the overall effect of the poem. In moments like these Chivers, despite his stylistic shortcomings, produced poetry that in its simplicity, religious spirit, and provincialism fulfilled some of the requirements of the so-called true American lyric that many exponents of a native literature at the time were demanding.

After three long, solemn elegies *The Eonchs of Ruby* would have bordered on the lugubrious if a fourth had been added; hence "The Lusiad" provides a welcome change of pace. The title has little to do with Luis de Camoens' work; it denotes instead a girl, Lucy, who is taught by the poet to blow tunes on an "eonch" shell. Mourning her loss seems less funereal, especially when the rhyme has an unintentionally whimsical effect:

> On the banks of Talapoosa,
>   Long time ago.
> Where it mingles with the Coosa,
>   Southward to flow—
> Dwelt the Maid I love, sweet Lucy!
>   Lucy, long time ago—
> Bringing Heaven to earth, sweet Lucy!
>   Lucy, long time ago.
>   Ah! who now can know

> How I loved the Maid, sweet Lucy!
>   Lucy, long time ago.[13]

Talapoosa and Coosa are two rivers located in Alabama, and Chivers'
use here to some critics seems to verge on the ludicrous. One of the
poet's strongest supporters, S. Foster Damon, has a low opinion of
"The Lusiad."[14] Perhaps Damon is correct in finding many of the
mataphors absurd, but some sections of the poem have a redeeming
charm:

> Like the plaintive voice, in Summer,
>   Of the Dove, low,
> When her melting heart doth murmur
>   Accents of wo
> For the mate that is torn from her—
>   (Golden in flow—)
> Were the words of my sweet Lucy,
>   Lucy, long time ago.
>   Ah! who now can know
> How I loved the Maid, sweet Lucy!
>   Lucy, long time ago.[15]

"The Lusiad" has been considered a parody of Poe's "The Haunted
Palace."[16] While the meter is trochaic in both poems,[17] there is
otherwise little similarity.

"Isabel; Ballad of Love" is a better example of the Chiversian
refrain. Love reveals its sensual side to the poet in lines more graceful
in movement than those of "The Lusiad:"

> When my head lay on the pillow
>   Of thy breast, dear ISABEL!
> Heaving like some milky billow—
>   Fare-thee-well!
> Then they heart gushed overflowing
>   From thine eyes too blind to see—
> Washing out the roses blowing
>   On thy cheeks—farewell to thee![18]

Chivers was an intelligent man, but, having traveled little, was at
times overwhelmed by the wonders of a big city. After attending a
concert in New York by Mme Caradori Allen he expressed his
reaction in the enthusiastic strains of "To Cecilia:"

> Like mellow moonlight in the month of June
> Waning serenely on some far-off sea,
> Died the soft pathos of that spiritual tune—
> Soft as the liquid hues of Heaven to me.[19]

Chivers provides an *explication de texte* for "liquid hues" by stating that it alludes "to the harmony between a soft sound and a blue color" in a manner reminiscent of Baudelaire's comment on his own poem.[20] The notion that all sense perceptions had the same basis or point of departure in a central function that correlated taste, feeling, smell, hearing, and vision, is traceable to Swedenborg who affected even the French Romantics prior to 1850. Another effort by Chivers to unify various sensory perceptions is made in "Lord Uther's Lament for Ella":

> By her side Cherubic Aster,
> With white limbs like alabaster,
> Circled through Heaven's azure pasture,
>   Half the fields of night to mow,
> When her heart to mine was given—
> Then she sang to me at even
> Golden melodies of Heaven
>   In the days of long ago.[21]

Effects achieved in rhyme and refrain in the descriptive terms in the above passage are put to good use. The cumulative result is a series of evenly cadenced and smoothly paced lines with few harsh and incongrous images to mar the overall impression of poems like "The Lusiad." Chivers arrives at a pleasing blend of poetically expressed concepts and music:

> On the green grass, passemented
> With the Eden-flowers, sweet scented,
> There she sits in Heaven, contented,
> With the Cherubs on the snow
> Of the flowers around them springing—
> Angels nectar to them bringing—
> Even shining, ever singing
>   Of the days of long ago.[22]

While discussing the subject of Chivers' esthetics, it is fitting to quote fully one short poem that sums up his thinking on religion and poetics:

THE SHELL

". . . It seems in truth the fairest shell of ocean."—SHELLEY

I.

What is it makes thy sound unto my ear
    So mournful, Angel of the mighty Sea?
Is it the soul of her who once was here,
    Speaking affection, through thy lips, to me?

II.

Oh! from my childhood this has been to me
    A mystery which no one could solve!—It sounds
And sorrows for the Sea incessantly—
    Telling the grief with which my soul abounds!

III.

Here, in its labyrinthine curve, it leaves
    The foot-prints of its song in many dyes;
And here, incessantly, it ever weaves
    The rainbow-tissue of its melodies.

IV.

When any harsher sound disturbs me here,
    In my lamentings in this world for thee,
I will apply it to my listening ear,
    And think it is thy soul come down to me.[23]

The shell in the Swedenborgian system of correspondences, as interpreted by Chivers, is an emblem of the arcana the poet alone is capable of fathoming. To Chivers, the shell also symbolizes the world of sensory impressions yet to be fully described by the poet; that realm is one in which music, the spoken word, and a painting can be united in their mutual expression of the beauty of the universe.

"The Dying Swan" at first seems a conventional piece until Chivers' vision of the end of the world comes into view. His imagination having been stimulated by Swedenborg's exegesis of the Apocalypse, Chivers in a succession of sounds and colors builds to a climax where the sonic effect of the words alone matters:

The cloud-sustaining, many-folded Hills—
 The soft, retiring mystery of the Vallies—
The open frankness of the verdant Fields—
 The winding Labyrinths of the emerald Alleys—
 The bending Heavens, with all the Stars in cycle sallies—
 The open mouths of Mountains—the dim Caves—
  Echoed her music with reverberant thunder,
 From their sepulchral throats—deep as the grave's—
  Dying around Night's throne now torn asunder—
  Leaving the rapt World mute with supernatural wonder!—[24]

Chivers tries to stimulate the reader's imagination to the point that he
furnishes sensations and impressions of sound and color to complete
further the word portrait of the universe's reaction to the Day of
Judgment. A cascade-like effect is derived from reading lines such as
the above. From time to time in *The Eonchs of Ruby* Chivers
succeeded in realizing new perspectives and in freeing poetry from
rigid and traditional patterns as he does in "Isadore," which is one
step further away from the grotesque verse of his contemporaries.
For obvious reasons, the poem figures prominently in the Poe-
Chivers plagiarism case:

> "Back to Hell, thou ghostly Horror!"
> Thus I cried, dear ISADORE!
> "Phantom of remorseless Sorrow!
> Death might from thee palor borrow—
> Borrow leanness ever more!
> Back to Hell again!—tomorrow
> I will go to ISADORE!"[5]

Politian's lament for Isadore recalls a haunting passage from "The
Raven." The strong similarity between the two poems forces students
of the controversy into separate camps; one claiming "Isadore" was
imitated by Poe in composing "The Raven"; the other stubbornly
refusing to concede that Chivers was anything more than a clever
copycat. At the very least, the extent to which both poets thought
along the same lines in terms of structure and use of the refrain is
striking. In conception and technique, they were ahead of most of
their contemporaries. Only in the orthodox theology preached in the
closing lines does Chivers clearly demonstrate one respect in which
they differed strongly. Poe was not overly concerned about the
ultimate destination of his lady friends, nor did he long to join them

after death in a Christian heaven; from this standpoint Chivers'
Politian is very unPoelike:

> ADON-AI! GOD OF GLORY!
>   Who dost love mine ISADORE!
>   Who didst hear her prayerful story
>   In this world when she was sorry—
>   Gone to Heaven forever more!
> ADON-AI! GOD OF GLORY!
>   Take me home to ISADORE![26]

Following right after the musicality and charm of "Isadore," the
choppy verse of "The Gospel of Love" is a sharp reminder of the ease
with which Chivers could lapse into mediocrity. One element makes
"The Gospel of Love" worthy of mention. It is one of the few poems in
which Chivers show definite signs of some social consciousness when
he deplores inadequate care for the insane:

> The madness we can not endure,
> We sent to Hospitals to cure—
> Purging the heart to make it pure
> From future ills to keep secure.[27]

A surprising modernness of perception on the problems of mental
health is coupled with a very progressive outlook on penal reform.
Chivers gives his unqualified disapproval of capital punishment, for
God alone bestows life on man and has the right to take it away:

> That which belongs alone to God,
> He has upon no man bestowed;
> Death-punishment, therefore, for good,
> Should be erased from penal code.[28]

The central idea of "The Gospel of Love" is the proper care of
children who should be reared by loving and tender parents. Chivers
might well have been thinking of some of his own children, taken
from him by untimely deaths, and of how he wuld have attended to
their needs with paternal solicitude had they lived. Social insights are
all very fine, but they have no place in a poem if they are not properly
expressed in an esthetically appealing style.

Chivers returns to better form in "Evening" when depicting the

effect of the sun's rays shining on rapidly flowing water and a school of
fish swimming in the current:

> Down in the acromatic streams,
> Meeting the luminiferous beams
> With which the air forever teems,
> The golden mail of minnows gleams.[29]

Equally effective is the panorama of the heavens in the initial stanza of
"The Chaplet of Cypress," an elegy written for one of his sisters,
Florence. Chivers again proves himself adept at creating the sensa-
tion of soaring through space:

> Up through the hyaline ether-sea,
> Star-diademed, in chariot of pure pain,
>   Through th' empyreal star-fires radiantly,
> Triumphant over Death in Heaven to reign
> Thy soul is gone, seeking its BLEST ABODE,
> Where break the songs of stars against the feet of GOD.[30]

Images in "The Chaplet of Cypress" that suggest realms above the
earth, "the hyaline ether sea" and "empyreal star-fires" raise the
reader's spirits. A tribute to Florence ends the poem and sets the
mood for the following "Threnody" dedicated to Chivers' son
Tommy:

> Ah! Angelic was my Tommy,
>   Tommy, Death has early slain.
> Tommy taken early from me!
> Whose sweet life did so become me,
> That his death doth now consume me—
>   Parching up my heart with pain!
> Ah! Angelic was my Tommy—
>   Never coming back again![31]

The pattern for the repetition of "Tommy" marks one of Chivers'
many attempts to achieve variety in rhythm and rhyme. At the
beginning of the second and third lines, the word which ended the
first line is repeated. Chivers probably meant to create the impression of funeral music with its steady repetitive beat.

Among the seemingly endless series of elegies about the death of his children, there is one that hints a vague reference to an earlier love, possibly his first wife; some of the unevenness typical of *The Path of Sorrow* remains. By picturing the party to whom the poem is addressed as already deceased, Chivers could conceal a reference to a living person. The wistfulness of the lines brings to mind the remorse voiced earlier over the rupture with his first love:

> I hear, at even,
> The liquid carol of the birds;
> Their music makes me think of thee in Heaven,
> It is so much like thy sweet words
> The brooklet whispers, as it runs along,
> Our first love-story with its liquid tongue.[32]

Poetry that would be of no consequence has at times a redeeming feature when Chivers adds a distinctive note that reflects his personal concerns whether he mourns the loss of loved ones or expresses his regionalism. This love of the homeland finds expression in mediocre poems, valuable only as evidence of Chivers' folklorism. "Song from the Inner Life" terminates in a stanza that has the rough and honest outlines of a Black spiritual or a hymn sung by the congregation of a Baptist Church. This poem resounds with Chivers' untutored impulse to portray the feelings and emotions associated with his youth and early manhood in Georgia, a reminder of the essentially frontier society in which he was reared: "Wide as Ezekiel's everflowing river, /No eye could see across it was so broad /Shall this sweet song flow down the world forever—The pure in heart see God.'[33]"From a moment of Baptist fervor Chivers with surprising adaptability turns to an improbable theme for a Southern Protestant of the mid-Nineteenth century, "Catholic Hymn to the Virgin:"

> Santa Maria! hear! oh! hear!
> And turn to me thy gracious ear;
> For thou art to the sorrowing near,
> And, to the Catholic ever dear![34]

Despite Chivers' limited contact with Catholicism and his innate fear of the papist threat, he gives a rather accurate picture of a devout Catholic praying to the Virgin to intercede with her Son. She is portrayed as a mediator and not as the Christian goddess depicted in many biased versions of Church teachings. The "Catholic Hymn to the Virgin" also figures prominently in the plagiarism controversy since it is compared to Poe's "Catholic Hymn."

On another theme, one which represents in a sense a different kind of religious experience, the "Song of LeVerrier on Discovering a New Planet" is an effort to relive the astronomer's emotions when confirming the existence of Neptune through mathematical analysis. Once again Chivers displays his ability to grasp the tremendous significance of infinity and virtually whirl his readers with him through space. By alliteration and metaphor he achieves a measure of sublimity. The general impact of the poem, unified and forceful, shows that Chivers' forte lies more in shorter poems and in isolated passages of longer works. His powers are more diffused in lengthier poems. While the following passage may appear commonplace, the turn of the phrase and the terms are strongly Chiversian:

> Floating in chariot of celestial fire,
>   Sphered Heavenward through the Empyreal Ether-Sea,
> He rays his sphere-tones out unto the choir
>   Of God until they fill Eternity.
> Tempestuous whirlwinds of deep melody
>   Dash from his orb-prow on his spheric road—
> Rolling in mountain-billows on Heaven's sea
>   Against the white shore of the feet of God.[35]

Chivers, striving for a degree of esthetic perfection, was intermittent and sporadic. Sublimity nestled side by side with mediocrity. Some portions of "Good Night" are definitely inferior although one stanza for sheer resonance and graphic quality would have few rivals in American poetry of the mid-nineteenth century:

> Here we both stand broken hearted,
>   Leaning on each other's heart;
> For in parting we seem parted,
>   Just to think that we must part.
> See! the pale, cold moon is waning—
>   Sinking softly from our sight—
> While our souls are here complaining
> For the loss of our good night!
>   Good night, my Love! my dearest!
>   High Heaven of my delight!
>   Of all things brightest, fairest!
>   My Beautiful—good night![36]

"The Voice of Thought" furnishes the reader with some clue to the inner world from which Chivers derived his moments of inspiration, both good and bad:

> Faint as the far-down tone
>   Beneath the sounding sea,
> Muffled, by its own moan,
>   To silent melody;
> So faint we cannot tell
>   But that the sound we hear
> Is some sweet roses' smell
>   That falls upon our ear;
>   (As if the Butterfly,
>   Shaking the Lily-bell,
>   While drinking joyfully,
>   Should toll its own death-knell!)
> Sweeter than Hope's sweet lute
>   Singing of joys to be,
> When Pain's harsh voice is mute,
> Is the Soul's sweet song to me.[37]

Once more, Swedenborg's views on the intermingling of sensory impressions shape Chivers' thinking as the poet attempts to convey his impression of immaterial concepts through specific physical sensations. In this instance thought has a voice and is compared to the fragrance of a rose. The notion of speech expressed through silence recalls some of Swedenborg's remarks on silence as one characteristic of angelic language. From this poem the reader can derive an image of Chivers' own internal state when composing poetry; as described by him, his spirit is like a combined sound chamber and flower bed filled with an aromatic music.

On the subject of poetic theory, Chivers had something in common with Poe in the use of the refrain and in the conjuring-up of sensory images. The mere coincidence that both poets used the same title for their respective poems need not produce speculation about possible plagiarism. Except for the title, there is little similarity between Poe's and Chivers' "Eulalie". The Georgian's mark is deeply imprinted on his own version in which his flamboyant imagery is redeemed by a certain gracefulness:

> Her rich cascade of hair,
>   Around her swan-like throat,
> Down on her bosom bare,

In wavy gold doth float.
Her lily-lidded eyes,
    Burning in her own light,
Seem melted from the skies,
    They are so Heavenly bright.
Her hands are rosy-white,
    Like lilies in the sun;
Her countenance makes bright
All that she smiles upon.[38]

The name of another young lady, "Lily Adair" inspires a poem that brings to mind, in its use of the repetend, two other poems by the Georgian, "Ellen Aeyre" and "Rosalie Lee." In "Lily Adair" the refrains, shortened and more compact:

Where the Opaline Swan circled, singing,
    With her cider-down Cygnets at noon,
In the tall Jasper Reeds that were springing
    From the marge of the crystal Lagoon—
Rich Canticles, clarion-like, golden,
    Such as only true love can declare,
Like an Archangel's voice in times olden—
    I went with my LILY ADAIR—
With my lamb-like LILY ADAIR—
With my saint-like LILY ADAIR—
With my beautiful, dutiful LILY ADAIR.[39]

Memories of Poe are invoked by the subject and refrain of "Lily Adair." If Chivers lacked Poe's level of performance, he was at least more often original in his philosophy and use of subject matter. Incapable of consciously indulging in the slavish imitation of any poet and deeply religious by nature, the ex-Baptist converted by Swedenborg combined the austerity of his childhood beliefs with the intriguing mysticism of the New Church. The concept of the spiritual body continuing humanlike in the celestial sphere fascinated Chivers. He yearned to communicate with angels in heaven, and he counted the steps in perfection necessary to achieve the closest possible union with God. In voicing his longing for the other life, Chivers sought objects in the physical world that were harbingers of things to come. This search resulted in a fusion of sensory images in keeping with Swedenborg's notion of the fundamental union of sensations. What was a useful poetic technique had a theological basis. Chivers was more consistent in one respect than poets merely interested in the esthetic advantages afforded by Swedenborg. A convinced disciple of the Scandinavian seer, the Georgian regarded his efforts in the lyric as an exposition of theological truth. In many poets, such an assumption would be judged unwarranted; in Chivers, the statement of his beliefs, whether in poetry or in prose, is clear and unequivocal. He was too ingenuous to indulge in ambiguous subtleties. From Swedenborg's revelations, he undoubtedly acquired the impulse to picture the heavens and man soaring through space. To Chivers the infinity of space mirrored divine omnipotence.

With a similar naiveté and brashness Chivers made no pretense of concealing his unaffected regionalism and provincial background. His very outlandishness stemmed from a frankly nationalistic as well as a Georgian orientation. Although grotesque imagery and devices in much of his poetry are perhaps best explained by his folkloric bent what constituted beauty to the popular taste apparently seemed appropriate to Chivers for poetry addressed to sedate readers of a cultivated society. Similarly, the reiterative and simple strains of Baptist hymns were to him fitting models for elegies or religious lyrics. As for his nationalism Chivers may have voiced his sentiments with less polish than Continental writers, but pride in one's country to the point of Chauvinism was fashionable in the nineteenth century.

The variation in the quality of Chivers' verse is understandable in terms of his own unpredictable and chameleonic temperament. He could write atrocious lines one moment and then compose a moving passage on the death of his children; such personal notes are endearing for their lack of affectation. Although seldom given to crusading in the cause of social reform, he could voice concern about injustices with a profound awareness of the ills of society.

Some poems in *The Eonchs of Ruby,* while providing justifiable grounds for speculation on the extent of Chivers' borrowing from Poe, frequently point only to aims and techniques common to both poets. A more profitable subject of inquiry would be the manner in which Chivers and Poe represented a unique trend in American poetry, one apart from the main current. Baudelaire, and later the French Symbolists, found much to admire in Poe. Chivers in *Eonchs of Ruby* also probed into the sonic effect of words divorced from their literal meaning, a technique to be developed in detail by Mallarmé and his school. As conventional as Chivers often was in the choice of thematic material, he still had, for a regional poet, unexpected and startling insights into the area of rhyme, meter, and imagery. For this reason the *Eonchs of Ruby* is often of interest to the literary historian.

CHAPTER 6

Atlanta

I *Preface*

A *tlanta: or the True Blessed Island of Poesy: A Paul Epic in Three Lustra*, first published in installments in the *Georgia Citizen* in January, 1853, shortly afterwards came out in pamphlet form. The verse romance has the same general story line as *Nacoochee* with the mysterious, remote island; the hero's journey there in a canoe, and the theme of quest for everlasting love and happiness. This time the Indian Chief Lamorah, to avenge the death of his son, Yanassa, has seized Ianthe and put her on an island to separate the maiden from her lover, Julian. Disguised as Yanassa returned from the dead, Julian outwits Lamorah and rescues Ianthe. The inconsequential plot actually serves as an allegory of the search for spiritual truth.

In the preface to *Atlanta*, Chivers repeats his intention to produce a poetry akin to music: "Now, as by changing the application of different flowers, a continual and ever varying regalement may be kept up in the organs of smell; so also, by the repeated applications of new and melodious imagery in a Poem—novel intonations in music—is the soul enabled to enjoy, while forever thirsting after, protracted delights."[1]

Lyric poetry, insisted Chivers, always raises the spirits by its musicality and constitutes an important phase of religious revelation. To the poet, the "illuminated Seer"[2], beauty appeared as it existed in its purest form in the ideal world which was imperceptible to the untutored eye. In a lyric poem "pleasurable impressions"[3] could be varied without ever allowing the reader to become bored. Chivers presented his exposition on esthetics primarily for a select group and not for the reading public at large: ". . . It is an experiment upon the minds of the *Chosen Few*, wrought out in order to introduce, for their consideration, a partial fulfillment of

77

the demands required by the souls of all true worshippers of the
Divine Beauty, as hinted at in the foregoing part of this Preface."[4]

Chivers envisioned the *"crystalline revelation of the Divine
Idea,"* being accomplished in *Atlanta.* In Swedenborgian fashion,
he refers to "Ministering Angels" who lead the "true Poet" to the
"way of all Beauty."[5]

II *Comparison with Poe's* The Poetic Principle

Written in 1842, the preface to *Atlanta* would seem to disprove the
contention of those who would trace Chivers' comments to Poe's *The
Poetic Principle.* Damon feels that any similarity between the two
writers' ideas would, in view of the fact that *Atlanta* was written
before *The Poetic Principle,* support Chivers' argument, in this case
at least, about the extent of Poe's indebtedness to him.[6] There are, of
course, substantial differences between the esthetic notions of
Chivers and those of Poe. The latter's were based primarily on an
intellectual perception of the beautiful and not on mystical insights
derived from Swedenborg, a point on which Chivers firmly insisted.
Poe, who scoffed at Swedenborg, would never accept Chivers'
premise that true poetry was one of the highest forms of religious
experience.

Similarities in thought and expression do invite a comparison of
The Poetic Principle with the preface to *Atlanta.* Chivers contends
that "no poem of any considerable length, form the very nature of the
relations subsisting between the power of the soul to receive, and the
impressions to be made, can be pleasing to any well-educated person
for any length of time."[7] In a still haughtier manner Poe states flatly,
"The value of the poem is in the ratio of this elevating excitement. . . . That degree of excitement, which would entitle a poem to
be so called at all, cannot be sustained throughout a composition of
any great length."[8]

On the subject of Milton's *Paradise Lost,* there is also a noteworthy
concurrence. "No person was ever yet pleased with the whole of
Milton's Paradise Lost nor, indeed, with any Epic of great length, the
beautiful or select passages only giving him delight,"[9] asserts Chivers
in a conclusion that brings to mind Poe's statement:
". . . There are, no doubt, many who have found difficulty in
reconciling the critical dictum that the 'Paradise Lost' is to be enjoyed
throughout, with the absolute impossibility of maintaining for it,

during perusal, the amount of enthusiasm which that critical dictum would demand."[10]

Both poets also agree that the epics of Homer's times were in reality a series of beautiful lyric passages and not a lengthy and tedious verse narrative. For this reason, Chivers insists that a poem, to be a "perfect specimen of the Art," must represent "an Epical Song" or a "melodious relation of an irrepressible yearning in the soul to unfold to itself its own intuitive longings after the Divine Beauty."[11] To Poe, however, musicality alone does not constitute the final criterion for a great poem: ". . . He who shall simply sing, with however glowing enthusiasm, or with however vivid a truth of description, of the sights, and sounds, and odours, and colours, and sentiments, which greet *him* in common with all mankind—he, I say has yet failed to prove his divine title."[12]

A more sublime goal is intended for the real poet in Poe's opinion, and it derives from a disciplined and polished style that incorporates an exquisite refinement in imagery and ideas. At this point, Chivers and Poe disagree. The Georgian was convinced that "novel intonations" and the effective repetition of "new and melodious imagery"[13] exemplified by the poetic devices in *Atlanta,* would result in sublime lyrics. A perusal of the comments by both poets leaves one unmistakable impression. Chivers was confident that, at a given moment, God would take over and apply the finishing touch to the work of art. Incapable of such reliance on heavenly intervention, Poe envisaged a beauty attainable solely by the talent and instinct of his own artistic genius.

Despite disagreement on the criterion for the end result, the perfect poem, Poe and Chivers still have much in common. Each one concedes the importance of sensory impressions and the intimate connection of music with poetry. Poe's refusal to accept musicality alone as a sufficient standard by which to judge the worth of a poem was quite a different matter from his perception of a more profound truth, the interrelationship of music and poetry.

An additional piece of evidence connects *The Poetic Principle* and the ideas expressed therein with Chivers' views. Poe brings up the question of Shelley's artistry and the pre-eminent position of Tennyson in English poetry, and may have mentioned these topics because they were considered in the literary discussions of the two American poets recorded in Chivers' projected biography of Poe. It is quite possible that their discussions included other subjects not covered in

Chivers' biography. Failure on Chivers' part not to explain to Poe the esthetic principles stated in the preface to *Atlanta* would have been most unusual especially since the Georgian was notoriously repetitious. Poe after listening to the Georgian explain the views later written in *Atlanta* may have been moved to consider some phases of Chivers' theory and to embody them eventually in an essay marked by his own personal touch. To say the least, this particular point in the Poe-Chivers controversy demonstrates that the question of plagiarism is one not readily solved.

III   *Analysis of* Atlanta

Glowing promises of poetic innovations made by Chivers in the preface were not fulfilled by the prosaic introduction of Ianthe, the heroine of *Atlanta,* as a rustic maiden.[14] When Lamorah kidnaps Ianthe, Julian pines for his sweetheart, a paragon of Chateaubriandesque and Swedenborgian ideals:

> Mourning that he could never more behold
> The beauty of her Angel-face, nor drink
> Delight again out of her heavenly smiles,
> Wherein his soul had sunned itself to peace.
> She was the Virgin of the first fond love.[15]

The first Lustrum, or canto, is a wearisome repetition of Chiversian commonplaces. Allusions to Swedenborgian teachings are juxtaposed with the tale of Lamorah, Count Julian, and Ianthe. The poet apparently never tired of using the threadbare plot of the two lovers threatened by vindictive Indians, variations of which can be read in *Nacoochee, Count Julian* and *Osceola.* Moreover, the second Lustrum starts out with the same Chateaubriandesque clichés: Lamorah mistakes Julian for the spirit of Yanassa returned from the dead, and the usual comments about the stoicism and majesty of the old chief in his woodland haunts are made; Julian, who later achieves a presumably higher state of spirituality, has no compunction about deceiving Lamorah. Julian's reunion with Ianthe is also devoid of moral tone; their love is consummated with unrestrained sensuality and passion. Somewhat more paradisiac is the description of "Eden Isle" where Ianthe resides:

> Looking like some great sea of molten gold
> (Like some great Emerald Mountain rising up)

> They saw the Eden Isle burst on their sight!
> The Hills, like some great Caravan encamped,
> At noontide, on the desert of the world
> Still billows of the World's great terrene sea
> As if they were the mighty groves of Gods
> The rising stepstones to the Deity
> Bristled with lofty pines, that in the distance looked
> Like mystic moss covering their purple backs
> Spread out in undulating lines afar
> Were deluged with rich radiance, as they lay
> Propping the thunder-clouds of Heaven, beneath
> The golden glory of the springing Sun
> Rising in such Empyreal pomp from out
> The Emerald splendor of the Eastern sea.[16]

Chivers furnishes an impressive picture of the landscape by selecting those details that enable the reader to visualize the scene in a primitive wilderness. Chivers retains his ability to carry over into verse a rather nice sense of perspective so that the eye takes in gradually the entire panorama starting with the treetops and ending in the limitless sky intermittently concealed by the clouds. Such charming passages compensate in great part for the defects in *Atlanta*.

The third Lustrum tells of a temple on Eden Isle which contains crystal formations that prefigure the absolute splendor of celestial beauty and that are probably intended to be a foretoken of Swedenborg's World of Spirits. While the amorous relationship of the two lovers continues unabated, they steadily assume a more spiritual tone as Chivers implies that they are now married in the eyes of God. Julian and Ianthe reenact the roles of Adam and Eve in a second Eden. Chivers' word power comes into play in a deliciously sensuous passage that depicts the luscious fruits of this earthly paradise which somehow seems located in the heart of Georgia:

> So when he woke, she fed him with her own
> Fair hands, on fruits plucked from the Eden-trees
> On golden luscious Nect'rines, Apples, Pears,
> And Mangoes, Yellow Plums, delicious Dates
> Conserve of Roses mixed with Damson Cheese,
>
> . . . .
>
> The golden grapes hung clustering in the sun,
> Oozing their luscious Nectar on the ground
> Rare vintage ripe of rich deliciousness
> Tempting the soul to eat continually.[17]

With a diet of organic food there are no longer any obstacles to spiritual progress. The love of Julian and Ianthe has now reached such a state of perfection that, while still on earth they are elevated to an angelic level, and they witness on Eden Isle the coming of the millenium:

> Thus did they realize the Golden Age
> In all its luxury of natural pomp
> Interpreting the Pythagorean dream
> Of man's perfectibility on earth.
> It was not sensual, but with mental love,
> That sweet Ianthe loved her Julian now
> Although that modified her spiritual love
> Giving such rapture to her soul;
> But such as Angels feel in loving God,
> Or one another pure celestial love
> For, in the Angel-meekness of her face
> The melting tenderness of her blue eyes
> He saw glimpses of that Celestial State
> Where Angels dwell in all their perfectness.[18]

The text speaks for itself, Chivers combines contemporary social Utopianism with the Swedenborgian scale of spiritual perfection. One earth Julian and Ianthe exemplify the perfectibility operable in man when given the opportunity to develop. Thus they have already realized a high level of celestial bliss. Like the angels of Swedenborg's heaven who enjoy a perpetual Sabbath in the spirit of truth and love before God, the two lovers experience a boundless joy. This "Celestial State," Chivers envisions in *Atlanta,* is much more than another Platonic allegory. Rather it is the application of the principles asserted in *Search After Truth.* As the poet-seer Chivers outlines the fulfillment of an Edenic order in the relationship of another couple in a paradise who, unlike Adam and Eve, have the advantages of guidelines laid down by Swedenborg.

Theological preoccupations did not make Chivers lose sight of his poetic mission in *Atlanta.* There is a basic melody to the blank verse maintained on an even key throughout the poem. An impression of life in this second garden of Eden occupied by Julian and Ianthe is transmitted by simple and direct lines:

> Beside the golden-sanded streams that ran
> Along the Violet Valley near the Cave,

> Whose crystal-fretted rich magnificence
> Did emulate the glory of the sky.[19]

Admirers of Chivers attest to the evocative quality of the metaphors and similes in *Atlanta*. The Georgian comes close to realizing here his ambition to communicate his concept of divine truth by using a series of sensations to provide the reader with an idea of the eternal. This idea, Chivers hoped, would result from a direct perception of beauty without an intermediate process of abstraction. The closing lines with their rather artless enumeration of precious gems have a cumulative quality that leaves the reader, for the moment at least, with the impression that he has caught a glimpse of a halcyon existence:

> Rich Rubies, Amethysts, Cornelian Stones,
> Bright Garnets, Jacinths, Emeralds, Almondines
> Take such sweet voluptuous delight
> With his ravishing Houri of the Isle,
> That his lost Paradise now seemed restored
> To him again with all its former joys,
> And they were two immortals living there,
> Filled with the plenitudes of boundless bliss.[20]

When read aloud, Chivers' poetry has the agreeable effect of the strains of a simple melody by no means sublime but capable of pleasing the reader, or auditor, for a brief period. This effect was the very one Chivers hoped to achieve:

. . . As all impressions are made upon the soul in time . . . it is obvious that no long-continued effort can last without a loss in those pleasurable sensations which are consequent upon freshness of nervous energy and always attend first impressions. It is, therefore, clear that no poem of any considerable length, from the very nature of the relations subsisting between the power of the soul to receive, and the impressions to be made, can be pleasing to any well-educated person for any length of time. The same may be said of music. This is the reason why Lyrical Poetry always has been, and always will be, pleasing to the soul.[21]

Chivers' words in the preface define his goals in *Atlanta*. Impressions received on the spot that illumine divine truths were what he sought to transmit directly to the reader. Granted the occasional lack of refinement in imagery and expression in *Atlanta*, the poem has not a few outstanding passages and a pervading vigor in imagery that atone for the interior lyrics of Chivers' earlier period. His claims to a role as innovator in the field of poetry are to some extent substantiated by *Atlanta*. A sensation of a luxuriant paradise with luscious fruit growing in abundance is attained with reasonable success in various parts of the work. Ianthe is a sex symbol by comparison to Nacoochee who remains undefiled by man. In the final analysis, unlike *Nacoochee,* a higher Swedenborgian ideal is achieved in *Atlanta*. A connubial union, begun in this life, frees itself of sensuality to approach a spiritual perfection that anticipates a state to be enjoyed on the celestial plane.

CHAPTER 7

Memoralia

I *Background of Publication and Preface*

*M*emoralia; or, Philas of Amber Full of the Tears of Love was printed as a giftbook by Lippincott in Philadelphia in 1853. Since giftbooks were popular at the time, Chivers probably hoped the current vogue would increase sales. A few copies did find their way into libraries and on the shelves of some prominent writers and critics, but the general reaction was unfavorable. Chivers should have anticipated such a reception, for *Memoralia* was nothing more than the *Eonchs of Ruby* to which twenty-six pages had been added. Except for the title page, index, and "The Vigil of Aiden," the *Enochs of Ruby* remained intact.

The preface of *Memoralia*, a florid restatement of ideas previously better expressed by Emerson in *Nature* and *Language*, is another Swedenborgian elucidation of the poet's role, calling, and function. "It is the natural outgushing of that intuitive perception of the influx of the divine life of God into his soul which constitutes true Poetry." To Chivers, the term "Gothic," when applied to lyric poetry, signified the "most ancient utterings of the God-inspired Prophets of the antediluvian ages," when man, still in an "Edenic state," conformed to God's will.[1]

While the Hebrews had a deep knowledge of divine beauty, they had worthy rivals in the Greeks who realized a most sublime art by "the Synthesis of the highest sensation united to the loftiest thought." This ideal of the Greeks was what Chivers meant by "a perfect unition of Art and Passion in any *crystalline Revelation* of the Divine Idea."[2] The distinction between the concept of beauty in Israel and that in Greece was clear in Chivers' mind. "While Taste sat as umpire of the Greek Beauty, the Moral Sense governed the Hebrew mind."[3] Chivers credited the Jews, as God's chosen people, with having a certain advantage on the moral plane sufficient to offset the great cultural tradition of the Greeks.

In the poem itself, declares Chivers, beauty assumes two aspects. "Just as there are in the Sacred Oracles, a spiritual and a
literal meaning," so is there "an outward and inward beauty" in the
poem.[4] Art, the external form, and Passion, the internal form,
enjoy the relationship of body to soul. The ideal poem, therefore,
would be a perfect combination of Art and Passion. The poet, able
to recognize the correspondences in nature, was the person emi-
nently qualified to achieve this union.

Chivers beholds in the female body the outer manifestation of
beauty and the material for the "Art" which the poet must join to
the inner spirit or passion in composing a sublime poem. The mark
of a true poet "depends entirely upon the power" to "express his
recognition of the Divine Beauty," which should always be "amen-
able to certain essential laws of Taste."[5]

Homer and Shakespeare rank high on Chivers' list of great
poets. In their works can be seen the quality Chivers calls "fortuitous" which he defined as "that which is co-eternal with the
creation of the Poetical Forms of Beauty—and co-existent with the
Revelation of the Divine Idea." A poet sensitive to the "fortuitous"
would "write his Poems in Rubies on a diaphonous Tablet of pure
Diamond;" and, "by the tender refinement of his soul," would
become "susceptible to the most delicate impressions."[6] The degree of inspiration experienced by the true poet is depicted by
Chivers in terms of the sensuous delights of luscious fruits and
fragrant flowers.

Chivers outlines here the main points in his individualistic system of esthetics. The preface to *Memoralia* is important in providing a definition of "Gothic fortuitousness" to which he alludes in
unpublished manuscripts on esthetics; this concept combines two
elements: the Gothic, or poetic spirit of Eden when man had close
communion with God, and the fortuitous, or the quality of poetry
that is a direct reflection of the divine exemplar. This definition is
essentially Romantic in spirit, but lip service is paid to taste and to
Classical concepts of ideality and purity. Passion for Chivers is a
strong emotional reaction to the universe and art, a form that relies
to a great extent on the personal whims of the individual poet. The
Georgian, who was too stubborn to kowtow to a prescribed set of
literary canons, also believed that a sacerdotal calling placed the
true poet in a world beyond the vision of the run-of-the-mill critic.

In Chivers' world of Swedenborgian symbolism rubies and
diamonds, emblems of perfect truth and love, signified the poet's

intimate comprehension of celestial verities.[7] The emotional intensity with which Chivers used these symbols renders more understandable his efforts to make poetry more than a complicated set of ideographs. Instead, the word was to be expanded to encompass more aspects of everyday life, and no facet of living was more important or common to man than that of the senses. Swedenborg had opened Chivers' eyes to a vast domain of hidden symbols to which the Georgian poet hoped to give expression.

II *Added Poems*

Although there is frequently a gap between a theory and its realization, "Bochsa," the first and the best poem of those added to the previous collection of *Eonchs of Ruby,* deserves notice. Dedicated to the famous harpist, Robert Bochsa, the opening lines of the poem present much of Chivers' favorite imagery:

> I knew an old man, Bochsa was his name,
> Fresh from the Mountain Morning Land, who came
> Into this Western Evening Land to charm us
> With his rich oversoul of musical lore—
> His polysongs of many sounds—tones learnt
> Not from the voices of the birds on earth,
> Nor any human speech—but heard in dreams—
> In interlunar swoons, when his rapt soul
> Drank inspiration, in the calm of night,
> Out of the crystalline bubbling Wells of God,
> Baptising us with dews of spiritual peace;
> From his reminiscences of the life
> He lived in Adam, when the World was young,
> And he was happy in the love of God;
> From Voices of the Nebilungen Land—
> From the influx of God's life into his soul—
> (Which was the fire Prometheus stole from Heaven—
> Burning therein rich songs of living fire,
> Like those the Seraphim heard at Eden's Gates,
> When the bright Morning Stars together sang,
> And all the Sons of God shouted for joy.[8]

Bochsa, the harpist, represented to Chivers a splendid example of "Gothic fortuitousness" at work. The "Pre-existent State" is at once Platonic and Swedenborgian. Through the harpist's ability to attain an Edenic frame of mind, he is capable of evoking many reminis-

cences of the World of Spirits. The influx of divine life enables the
musician to achieve on his instrument effects also produced by the
poet. Possibly there was a latent elitism in Chivers that expressed
itself in esoteric theosophy and an exclusive concept of esthetics.
Sounds and sights beyond the ken of normal men, unused to
"interlunar swoons," were perceived by the Georgian when con-
templating the after-effects of Bochsa's concert. The result is a
striking and provocative series of word combinations that somehow
reach a certain loftiness of tone in a manner more characteristic of
Symbolism than Romanticism.

In verse more traditional in nature, Chivers is on occasion guilty of
monotonous cadence and tedious rhythm. He was more apt to put his
best efforts into a poem like "Bochsa," whose theme was more
challenging. "The Poet" is the only other selection among the new
works in *Memoralia* that has a true Chiversian spark:

> The Poet, through all things on earth, can see
> Glimpses of that Celestial State to be.
> The Voices of all Ages, from their dim
> Abodes, (his foregone echoes,) answer him.
> God's holy Messenger to ignorant men
> To lead them safely back to Heaven again;
> For that Celestial State is far above
> This low, terrestial one in heavenly love.
> He is the Echo of great Nature's voice,
> Whose utterance makes the heart of Man rejoice—
> That God-made Memnon who dost ever make
> Celestial music for his own soul's sake;
> Thus he becomes the prophet of all time,
> Archangel-like, in thunderous tones sublime—
> Preaching that mystic music unto men,
> Which Angels shall rehearse in Heaven again.
> Then listen to him while he sings to thee
> Of what thou art—what thou shalt surely be;[9]

In "The Poet," Chivers summarizes the essential ideas in his preface
to *Memoralia;* the poet's effort to write celestial lines will be repeated
by angels in the Swedenborgian heaven. Perhaps Chivers envisioned
some of his contemporaries reciting his poems in paradise. Especially
significant is the allusion to the poet's "glimpses" of the "Celestial
State" which suggests that Chivers was probably convinced that his
spirit would now and then, like Swedenborg's, leave the body and
pay a brief visit to heaven.

CHAPTER 8

Virginia *and Final Works*

I *Background of Publication and Analysis of Preface*

V*irginalia; or, Songs of My Summer Nights* was printed at Philadelphia in 1853 by Lippincott. This time Chivers did not use one lengthy poem as the principal selection to which a collection of shorter lyrics was appended. Instead, almost all the poems were under two hundres lines in length. About one-half of them had previously appeared in magazines. A few commentators perceived some merit in Chivers' latest work, but the Georgian was, nonetheless, the recipient of the usual caustic remarks that greeted any new volume he dared to publish.

As was his custom, Chivers expounds in the preface the philosopical and esthetic notions central to *Virginalia*. Swedenborg's use of the polished diamond to symbolize heavenly truths is adapted by Chivers to fit his own theory of the preternatural function of poetry as an expression of divine truth:

> Now, you may as well tell me that a rough Diamond, newly dug out of the mines in Golconda, can be made the Mediator of the revelation of as much purely white light from the sun, as one that has been anointed to the office by the ingenuity of the Lapidary, as to tell me that any Poem can become the mediation of the influx of the Divine Life of God into the soul, without the highest knowledge of the true Art of musical language in the Poet—for just as the first owes its ability to express itself crystallinely to the peculiar mode of that cutting which is best calculated, according to the highest mathematical laws appertaining to the full development of light through a multiplication of highly polished facets—so does a full manifestation, or Shekinization, of the passions and emotions of the soul depend entirely upon the Art displayed in its creation, according to certain musical laws, by the Poet.[1]

Diamonds to Swedenborg were the emblems of celestial love; the successive degrees of color and the varieties of refraction in a diamond corresponded to the different phases of good and truth in heaven. The diamond also stood for spiritual light for, as Swedenborg explained, the influx of light into a diamond had a correspondential relationship to the supreme degree of spiritual life a soul could receive. The "crystalline revelation of the Divine Idea" is, as stated previously, Chivers' reference to the mystical sense attributed to crystal by Behmen and Swedenborg. For the Swedish mystic, this transparent substance connoted the shining light of divine truth as well as those believers who dwell in the knowledge which that light provides.[2] To Chivers any revelation to the poet of God's will furnished special insights into supernatural secrets hidden from ordinary mortals; to verify this point, he discourses on the function of the repetend in mystical terms:

"Now in regard to the Refrain of a Poem I merely mention here, that is is not only an ornament, but . . . an immortal soul, not a mere profane appendage, but a sacred Symbolical Ensignium . . . a diamond of glory, like the Urim and Thumnin on the Breastplate of the High Priest—or, those beautiful golden bells which jeweled the hem of his garment—making a pleasant chime . . ."[3]

II Analysis of Selected Poems

The refrain already appears in the first poem "Chactas; or, the Lament of the Harmonious Voice" which bears the explanatory caption "Founded on Chateaubriand's Atala." In the poem Chivers concentrates largely on increasing the suspense until the moment when Chactas is rescued by a strange Indian maid:

> The night arrived. The pale Moon seemed to glide,
> Weeping through Heaven, like Sorrow by my side—
> When lo! before me, swaying down the grass,
> A Maiden, beautiful as Heaven, did pass,
> With noiseless steps, upon the silver sands,—
> Then, turning round, untied my fettered hands!
> It was CELUTA! Angel of my heart!
> With whom, rejoicing, I did then depart!
> For blessed, blessed, blessed was the day
> When Chactas came from Pensacola Bay.[4]

One poem in the collection, "Ganymede," marks a continuation of another preoccupation typical of Chivers. The subject, he claimed, was based on an actual experience. Impelled by a mysterious

impulse, he had climbed to the heights of a hill and at the summit had
a vision of George Washington and the future greatness of America.
The crowning point of his revery is the realization of the supernatural
character of his vision:

> For Beauty, with her love divine,
> Intoxicates the soul like wine.
> Thus, glory-crowned, in robes of light,
> He soared up from the World's dark night.
> And sitting on the highest Sills,
> With Angels, on the Eternal Hills,
> Hears Heaven's immortal music roll
> Down God's great Ages through his soul.
>   Te Deum Laudamus![5]

Less inspired moments are handsomely redeemed by "Apollo,"
recognized by Bayard Taylor as one of the best poems in *Virginalia;*
he was especially impressed by the imagery in the third and sixth
lines of the following stanza[6]:

> Like some deep, impetuous river from the fountains everlasting,
> Down the serpentine soft valley of the vistas of all Time,
> Over cataracts of adamant uplifted into mountains,
> Soared his soul to God in thunder on the wings of thought Sublime,
> With the rising golden glory of the sun in ministrations,
> Making oceans metropolitan of splendor for the dawn—
> Piling pyramid on pyramid of music for the nations—
> Sings the angel who sits shining everlasting in the sun,
> For the stars, which are the echoes of the shining of the sun. [7]

Unlike other poems with only a few good passages, "Apollo" conveys
an even, sustained impression. The rough edges have been smoothed
and the result is an excellent short poem of three stanzas with
polished meter and rhythm. Noticeably absent is the far-fetched
imagery in which he was usually inclined to indulge.

"Lily Adair," while longer in length, has much the same quality as
"Apollo"; in addition the terminal rhyme scheme, *d-d-d-d* is
employed adroitly to enhance the musicality of the stanza. Chivers
also displays finesse in merely hinting at the general outlines of
maidenly comeliness:

> Thus she stood on the arabesque borders
> Of the beautiful blossoms that blew

> On the banks of the crystalline waters,
>   Every morn, in the diaphane dew.
> The flowers, they were radiant with glory,
>   And shed such perfume on the air,
> That my soul, now to want them, feels sorry,
>   And bleeds for my Lily Adair—
> For my much-loved Lily Adair—
>   For my long-lost Lily Adair—
> For my beautiful, dutiful Lily Adair.[8]

Like "Lily Adair," "Valete Omnia" also enjoys a sustained harmony thanks to the absence of any awkward metaphors. Another notable feature is the refrain which is reminiscent of previous ballad-like verse written by Chivers in which he successfully combines his musical and folkloric insights:

> The great golden hand on the Adamant Dial
> Of the Clock of Eternity pauses in Heaven!
> From Death's bony hand I now empty the Phial—
> And the Morning is just like the Even!
>   I go where the wild Roses blow
> On the banks of that Beautiful River whose flow
>   Is under the grave below!
>   All under the grave below!
> Then, farewell, father! farewell, mother!
> Farewell, sister! farewell, brother!
> I go where the wild Roses blow
>   All under the grave below![9]

"The Fall of Usher," criticized for its obvious Poe-isms, was written as a tribute to Chivers' late colleague. Borrowings from Poe were, therefore, both understandable and justifiable. To Chivers' credit he did not join the current trend to demean the dead writer but paid him just tribute:

> Thou art gone to the grave! thou art silently sleeping
>   A sleep which no sorrow shall ever molest;
> And, in longing for which, my poor heart now is keeping
>   This silent lament in its grave in my breast!
>   Like Shelley for Keats, in its grave in my breast![10]

Unlike the better poems in this collection, "Rosalie Lee" marks Chivers' lapse into the old habit of wildly choosing metaphors and of displaying almost complete disregard for common sense. What botanist has discovered cucumbers growing on a tree or, for that matter, how many poets compare that succulent vegetable to a goblet?

> Many mellow Cydonian Suckets,
>   Sweet apples, anthosmial, divine,
> From the Ruby-rimmed Beryline buckets,
>   Star-gemmed, lily-shaped, hyaline—
> Like that sweet golden goblet found growing
>   On the wild emerald Cucumber-tree—
> Rich, brilliant, like Chrysopraz blowing—
>   I then brought to my Rosalie Lee—
>   To my lamb-like Rosalie Lee—
>   To my Dove-like Rosalie Lee.—
> To my beautiful dutiful Rosalie Lee.[11]

Although referring once more to "Cydonian Suckets," the title "Pas d' Extase" suggests that his poem was gaily jotted down after seeing a company of ballerinas perform. Various Chiversian elements are combined in what begins like a sybaritic ditty and ends in the ecstatic ascent of the poet's soul to heaven. Chivers employs mythological imagery with the zest and vigor of a Georgian farmer who derived lusty enjoyment from his Classical studies. References to revelry and the imbibing of alcoholic spirits are a souvenir of earlier poems. Allusions to the deathbed recall the elegies to deceased loved ones. The closing lines are a reminder that, deep in the poet's subconscious, lay the hope of salvation. Quoted here in its entirety is a stimulating example of Chivers' feverish brain at work:

Pas d'Extase.

> Like those sweet Cydonian Suckets
> Hebe brings in crystal Buckets
>   To the Gods in Heaven above,
> When they drink, forever quaffing
>   Fiery draughts of living wine—
> Sometimes shouting, sometimes laughing
>   With the heavenly bliss divine;
> Was my soul made drunk with gladness—
> Rapt with most exultant madness—
>   Joy so sweet it turned to wo—
> Drinking down thy songs of sweetness

From thy heart's divine completeness,
   As if Heaven should overflow;
Like the Angel's heavenly laughter
Which the Gods go sighing after—
   Such as Gods alone can know;
Or the rapture of deep anguish
   Of some saintly soul when dying,
On his death-bed left to languish—
   Unto God forever crying—
When, amid his desolation,
Comes the news of his salvation,
   And his soul ascends up flying
Into Heaven with exultation—
   Like the Angels on the Ladder
Up from Bethel-plain at even;
   So my soul clomb [sic] gladder, gladder,
On the rounds of song to Heaven—
   Piled in incense from thy bosom,
Like the odor, late at even,
   From some Eden fresh in blossom.
When the world looks white as Heaven![12]

By its energy and vitality, "Pas d' Extase" provides a striking study
of Chivers. Several motifs are once more combined; what seemed a
bacchanalian revelry in a provincial Georgian setting is slowly
transformed into a mystical anticipation of celestial joys in the
afterlife. The immediacy of angelic presences quickens the poet's
sensation of climbing a ladder that leads to heaven.

As in "Cydonian Suckets," Chivers' ability to picture humble flora
and fauna in unusual, original terms is demonstrated in "Bessie Bell."
Few poets would speak of the action of a butterfly's wings as
"psychical," but Chivers does so because of his spiritualist view of
nature. The stanza quoted below has one of several references to
Israfel that caused Poe's constituents to suspect plagiarism; the
meter, nevertheless, has also been traced to the four-stressed
trochaic of Tennyson's "Locksley Hall." While Chivers might have
imitated the British poet in using this particular meter, the imagery
and subject matter are undeniably his own:

   Like the psychical vibration
      Of the BUTTERFLY'S soft wings,
   Dallying with the rich CARNATION—
      Played her fingers with the strings.
   Israfelian in its dearness—

All her heart's deep love to tell—
Bell-like, silver in its clearness,
Fell the voice of BESSIE BELL.[13]

The death of Henry Clay prompted Chivers to compose "Morcia Funebre," in which he achieved striking results in verbally reproducing the pealing of the bells. The very words by their strength and resonance reproduce the action of the alternate strokes of the clapper hitting the sides of the bell. Chivers borrowed from Poe's "The Bells"; but, unlike that poem, "Morcia Funebre" is more thunderous and resounding in its effects:

Toll, toll, toll!
Let your great Thor-hammer strike upon the bell,
Crushing from out his iron heart the dole—
To sable all the world with his funeral knell!
For the passing into glory of his soul—
For the Requiem of the soaring into glory of his soul!
Then toll, toll, toll!
Till the billows of your moan,
From your iron heart that inwardly doth groan, groan, groan,
Shall, like raging seas, roll on, on, on,
To the Goal, to the Goal—
To the glorious golden Goal—
Where that mighty Man is gone—
To the Kingdom of the Soul—
From this Valley of Dark Shadows to the Kingdom of the Soul![14]

At times Chivers put aside his ingrained provincialism to view the world on a wider scale. When surveying the situation in Europe, he could not resist the impulse to proclaim America the leader of freedom and the model to be emulated by enslaved peoples, even though, ironically, he himself was a slaveholder. There is a pre-Whitmanic strain in Chivers' vision of the United States' role and the sense of manifest destiny. While only a faint suggestion of Whitman's mighty lines is found in Chivers' "The Rising of the Nations," his poem foreshadows some of the pageantry of *Leaves of Grass*:

Now louder than the loud tumultuous Ocean
Stormed into passion by the ever-roaring Winds—
Come the loud shouts from all those-multitudes in motion,
Chorusing the lightnings of these million mighty minds—
Answering the Bugle-blasts from out the Mountains,

> Blown from the lips of ever-living Liberty—
> Louder than thunders of ten thousand fountains
> Leaping down cataracts of Adamant exultingly
> Impatient to become the Children of the Sea!
> So did these living Columns of the indignant Free,
> Sweep onward to the Angel-voice of Liberty,
> Over the desperate cataracts of Anarchy,
> Down to the opening Ocean of their Destiny—
> Piling their rafts of slain along the vallies,
> Like fallen forests—prostrate Monuments of slaughter—
> To fatten Earth, or fill up Buzzard's bellies—
> For future Tyrants, now, shall know no quarter![15]

In *Virginalia*, Chivers' poetic principles are put into practice with fair success. Romanticism is present in subjects carried over from previous works; Chateaubriandesque Indians, patriotic fervor, outbursts of melancholy, and glorification of feminine beauty all remind readers of Chivers' conventional side. To these elements might also be added a continuing interest in folklorism, ballads, and nature; the latter factor serves as a link between Chivers' conformity to prevailing Romantic vogues and a solitary search for a deep Swedenborgian meaning in the universe. This religious search, tightly bound to a quest for a new poetics, comes closer to realization in *Virginalia* than in previous works.

Chivers sets out to accomplish what he considers is his mission, the development of poetry as an instrument of sonority, in a physical as well as intellectual sense. At times, this results in poems that, when read aloud, produce a series of irregularly recurring impulses painful to hear. Quite often, however, Chivers literally generates a sustained vibrational energy from felicitous word combinations that convey to the reader not only ideas alone but impressions and sensations that bring into play all the reader's faculties; mind, imagination, and intuition are simultaneously stimulated. In striving for this goal Chivers shared a common bond with Poe and Lanier. Sonority and resonance were a characteristic, in fact, of nineteenth-century Southern verse.

III   *Miscellaneous Writings*

Birth-Day Song of Liberty *and* The Sons of Usna

In 1855 Chivers left the North never to return. The slavery issue could have influenced his decision to go back to Georgia; for, once on home ground, he lost no time in expressing his political and social views. Chivers' sectionalism was unequivocal, and he foresaw the day when the Northerners would force Georgia and her sister states to withdraw from the Union. The patriotic sentiments uttered so ardently and frequently in the past by Chivers moved a group of local citizens in Washington, Georgia, to ask their poet in residence to compose a poem for a Fourth of July celebration in 1856. Unable to comply with that time schedule, Chivers did subsequently write *Birth-Day Song of Liberty: A Paean of Glory for the Heroes of Freedom.*

Published in Atlanta in 1856 by C.R. Hanleiter, the poem is a lacklustre summary of the deeds of leading figures in American history that ends with a florid eulogy of the Lord's selection of the United States to play a crucial part in the divine strategy to ultimately spread democracy throughout the world. The anapests used by Chivers to produce an explosive and hammerlike effect only make the poem all the more reiterative and tedious. Conspicuously absent were the vigor and inventiveness of the *Eonchs of Ruby.*

After the Chauvinistic outburst in *Birth-Day Song of Liberty* the Georgian turned to quite a different subject derived from an old Irish legend. Chivers must have become acquainted with Theophilus O'Flanagan's *Daidra, or, The Lamentable Fate of the Sons of Usnach*[16] through a footnote to Thomas Moore's *Irish Melodies.*[17] Probably in about 1845 Chivers read O'Flanagan's translation of the Deidre legend; at any rate he had *The Sons of Usna* ready for publication in 1854. By now Chivers, who expected little support from editors was as usual reconciled to paying the printing cost; in 1858 C. Sherman and Son in Philadelphia were engaged to publish *The Sons of Usna.*

There is little merit to Chivers' exaggerated version of the tale of Deidre and the Usnas. Amusing attempts to imitate Shakespearean dialogue show that Chivers had made little progress since *Conrad* and *Eudora.* Possibly the first modern writer to treat the Deidre legend he still vitiates his work with pointless changes and additions when a poetic version of the main outlines of the old Irish tale might have resulted in at least an acceptable narrative poem like *Atlanta.*

The flaws of *The Sons of Usna* are present to a much greater extent in Chivers' other plays in the manuscript collection at Duke University Library. *Leoni, or the Orphan of Venice* is a preposterous attempt to stage the Kentucky Tragedy in Italian trappings. *Tacon* is a forgettable effort to dramatize the suffering of Cuba under Spanish domination. *Osceola* and *Count Julian*, both plays on the American Indian, are inferior to *Nacoochee* and *Atlanta* in their version of the Chateaubriand interpretation of the redmen. Similarly *Charles Stuart*, *Alba Regalis*, and *The Signet Ring* are best left in manuscript form. All of Chivers' unpublished plays lack even the documentary value of *Conrad and Eudora*.

CHAPTER 9

Chivers' Life of Poe *and the Poe-Chivers Controversy*

I *Background of Composition*

AS stated earlier Poe's relations with Chivers formally began in 1840 when he sent the Georgian an outline of a proposed periodical to be entitled *Penn Magazine*. When Chivers arrived in New York in the summer of 1845 to arrange for the publication of *The Lost Pleiad*, he finally met Poe. After their meeting, Poe gave *The Lost Pleiad* a favorable review in the *Broadway Journal*. Chivers returned to Georgia and never saw Poe again, but they kept up a correspondence with one another.[1]

Shortly after the death of Poe, Chivers had a brief literary dispute with those who accused him of plagiarizing "The Raven" and other poems. Although Chivers in reply claimed the opposite was true and that Poe had taken ideas from him, he still made no insidious attack on the hapless writer, similar to the diatribes of Rufus W. Griswold, a mediocre critic of Poe for whom Chivers had little use. In planning a manuscript of Poe's life, Chivers prepared to answer Griswold's attacks on Poe's character and reputation and to undertake a work he felt sure some publisher would accept. Though Poe's friends supplied him with papers, Chivers never succeeded in selling his manuscript to an editor.[2] The *Life of Poe* remained unpublished in the Henry E. Huntington Library until it was edited by Richard Beale Davis and published by E. P. Dutton in 1952.[3]

II *Summary and Analysis*

Chivers charitably overlooks Poe's alcoholism to extol his friend's intellect and literary powers. Brushing aside Griswold's remarks against Poe, Chivers leans over backwards to prove that Poe's apparent irreligion was the mask of a person capable of faith and even pictures him borne up to heaven in a chariot in keeping with Swedenborg's symbolic description of the preferential treatment given by God to select individuals.

One of the most valuable parts of Chivers' biography is the section devoted to his discussions with Poe about English writers. Both could agree on the general merits of Shelley and Keats, but agreement on Tennyson was a different matter. To Poe, the perfect poem required the inspiration of a writer of Tennyson's calibre who, Poe felt, for purity of form ranked even above Shelley. An irritated Chivers retorted that Tennyson was a womanish poet whose prettified verse did not measure up to acceptable esthetic standards. Of course Chivers had his own system of esthetics in mind. Poe replied contemptuously that a true poem would stand or fall on its intrinsic value. Both poets did agree in general on the principle that subtle and frequent alternations of rhythm, imagery, and harmony were best realized in a short poem. They still remained far apart, on the definition of poetic inspiration. What Poe deemed simply an elevation of the keenest faculties of the mind in the perception of beauty was for Chivers a mystic and supernatural experience in which the poet received directly from God a revelation of a particular aspect of the beautiful.

On a more mundane plane there was further difference of opinion on fellow writers; Poe had praise for James Russell Lowell, but Chivers dismissed him as commonplace. He accepted Poe's denunciation of Bryant since the Georgian disliked most of the New York literati. His reaction was one of shock and disbelief when Poe not only excoriated Shakespeare but, in a swift analysis of other British writers, assigned to oblivion Byron, Wordsworth, Coleridge, and Southey. Some of Poe's sallies may have been prompted by a mischievous desire to ruffle his staid companion. In his own critical articles, Poe on the whole, was less severe with the writers whom he took to task in Chivers' presence.

The exchange of literary views between Poe and Chivers, while of interest, is not the only worthwhile feature of the biography. Further details are given on the relationship between the two poets. There is ample evidence that Poe's occasional complaints about Chivers' stinginess were not a serious obstacle to their friendship. In the biography Chivers refers to a liaison Poe was having with a lady in Providence who answers to the description of Fanny Osgood.

Valuable data are also furnished on Poe's confrontation on a New York street with a hostile critic, Lewis Gaylord Clark, editor of the *Knickerbocker Magazine*. His cockiness bolstered by alcohol, Poe was ready to engage in fisticuffs. As an eyewitness, Chivers prevented the brawl Clark also wished to avoid. More peaceful is the Georgian's description of a visit to the cottage at Fordham that supplies interesting sidelights on Poe's home life there. The biography of Poe is in the main factual and informative. From the exchange of literary views students interested in Chivers and Poe may derive much useful information.

III *Background of the Poe-Chivers Controversy*

It is difficult today to have an adequate conception of the many storms of protest and bitter debates caused by plagiarism, deliberate or unintentional, in the nineteenth century. British reviewers were always quick to accuse American writers—generally scorned as semiliterate cousins from the wilderness—of pilfering ideas and imagery from a superior literature produced in England. One such reviewer, John Forster, sternly observed, "True poetry imitates nature; that which imitates poetry ought to have another name." American poets especially were guilty of what Forster termed "petty larceny . . . a prominent and ostentatious feature" of the mediocre verse ground out by hacks in the United States.[14]

Poe, in the main, agreed with Forster's criticism; but his own position on plagiarism was frequently ambivalent. He could not draw the line consistently between the author guilty of outright literary theft and the writer who was honestly inspired by the style, imagery, and ideas of one of his peers. In theory, Poe's stand on plagiarism was quite severe; to him contemporary literature presented no "more sickening spectacle than that of the plagiarist, who walks among mankind with a erecter step, and who feels his heart beat with a prouder pulse" and takes pride in the "plaudits which he is conscious are the due of another." To understand fully the seriousness of plagiarism, it was necessary, Poe reminded his readers in "The Literati" to contrast "the ethereality of just fame" and "the grossness of the crime of theft."[15] Poe, who did not always adhere to a strict interpretation of his own principles, admitted there were exceptions; but he was seldom charitable in his frequent claims about having evidence of flagrant plagiarism in Longfellow's works.

With such an unyielding attitude towards anything even approaching literary theft, it is not difficult to picture a sensitive and prideful Chivers taking umbrage at the slightest suggestion that he had been a callous plagiarist in borrowing freely from the style, subject matter, meter, refrains and imagery of Poe, a writer he claimed as a close friend. So convinced were the critics accusing Chivers' of plagiarism that the charges, which went largely unanswered, were associated with the Georgian well into the present century. Only recently has there appeared any willingness to concede that Chivers to some extent had a certain genius and originality.

Chivers' initial contact with Poe took place in 1831—if the Georgian is correct in stating that he read the volume of Poe's verse which was published in that year. Since Chivers was an assiduous reader of current magazines and newspapers, he was bound to have seen or read Poe's work in the *Southern Literary Messenger* and many other journals. In the meantime during the 1830's Poe read some of Chivers' poems; he later wrote to Chivers about "some imperfect recollections of one or two poems sent to the first volume of the *Southern Literary Messenger*,"[6] presumably in 1834 or 1835 when Poe was a critic for the magazine. As already seen, the two poets did not have any direct contact until the 1840's; prior to that time Poe most likely was familiar with *Nacoochee* which had a fairly wide circulation, but probably did not read either *The Path of Sorrow* or *Conrad and Eudora* because of their limited distribution. What can be established is Poe had some knowledge of Chivers as a writer in 1840, and looked favorably upon *The Lost Pleiad*.

The exact nature of their relationship is still subject to conjecture. Did Poe merely consider the Georgian an easy mark and the potential source of ready funds? If so, he soon discovered Chivers kept the purse strings securely tied. What was Chivers' interest in maintaining the friendship—just the privilege of referring to a distinguished associate? Since Chivers' loyalty to Poe following the latter's death refutes such a supposition, it is far more reasonable to assume that their relations were characterized on the whole by a substantial degree of mutual respect. The subsequent furor over plagiarism involving both poets is easily separable from their personal association thanks to Chivers' refusal to attack Poe's standing as a writer.

There is little question that the two poets recognized—without any mention of plagiarizing—that they both used similar methods and imagery. For about eight years they corresponded amicably. In light of their resemblance in taste and temperament, it is readily understandable that Chivers could unconsciously borrow from Poe and vice versa. Today critics and writers are less inclined to accuse someone of plagiarism, a charge that is often difficult to prove. Moreover, the act of plagiarizing is seldom a simple matter of a literary theft perpetrated with malice of forethought. More complex factors enter into the picture. How can one demonstrate that an apparent plagiarism is not in reality an unconscious homage rendered by a young writer, for example, to an older one who has exercised a profound influence on him? The same psychological elements must be taken into consideration in the Poe-Chivers controversy where the temperamental Georgian remained silent on the issue of plagiarism during Poe's lifetime when the facts of mutual borrowing were plainly in evidence. Only after Poe's death did Chivers suddenly burst forth with wild charges that the author of "The Raven" had copied his work and was endebted to him for many a lesson in the fundamentals of poetic technique. It should be noted that Poe made claims to originality only on the basis of the manner in which various components were assembled in his verse.

Chivers set off the literary debate by a chance remark in the *Georgia Citizen* of 1850 that Poe had imitated him.[7] The following year in 1851 Chivers asserted that "The Raven" owed much "To Allegra Florence in Heaven."[8] In the *Waverly Magazine* Chivers rejected the notion that Poe was responsible for remarkable innovations in poetic style and technique. (Under the pen name "Fiat Justitia" Chivers hid his identity rather ineptly to praise his own poetry.) If "The Raven" electrified the reading public by its novelty, the reaction was understandable observed "Fiat Justitia"; however, Dr. Chivers, and not Poe, first used "trochaic catalectic" in "To Allegra Florence in Heaven." The lines "Holy Angels now are bending" inspired the better known "Once upon a midnight dreary." Likewise the celebrated refrain "Nevermore" could be read in "Lament on the Death of My Mother" published in 1829 in the journal *Sentinel and Witness*. If Chivers had stopped at this point, he might have won a few supporters from the anit-Poe group. Unfortunately, "Fiat Justitia" insisted on quoting the ridiculous verse on the broken egg to clinch the case against "The Raven" as a patent imitation of Chivers.[9] This infelicitous choice alone was sufficient to prejudice even the least skeptical reader.

Previous to the article in the *Waverly Magazine*, Chivers had been brooding about hints from more than one critic that many passages in *Eonchs of Ruby* had been filched from Poe. Seeking support from fellow writers, on April 10, 1852, Chivers wrote to William Gilmore

Simms. "I am the Southern man who taught Mr. Poe all these things."[10] He asserted to Augustine Duganne on December 17, 1850, that "Poe stole every thing that is worth anything from me."[11] When corresponding with Rufus Griswold on March 28, 1851, Chivers complained that Poe "no doubt felt piqued when I accused him of having stolen his 'Raven' from my Poem 'To Allegra Florence in Heaven'."[12]

Such bold assertions by Chivers did not go unanswered. Henry S. Cornwell and J. J. P. replied in Poe's defense with two articles in the *Waverly Magazine*. Cornwell quoted a ditty, purportedly from the Cheshire, England, *Herald*, that had the refrain "Nevermore" to rebut Chivers' claim to being the first poet to capitalize on its inherently haunting quality; the egg simile is also waved aside with Homeric laughter, "an eggs-traordinary verse." *J.J.P.* joined the attack by concentrating on Poe's achievements despite the curse of alcoholism.[13] Neither writer offers a substantive refutation of "Fiat Justitia's" charges. The debate between Chivers and his two antagonists continued in the *Waverly's* pages. Although further examples were cited by Chivers to disclose the extent of Poe's endebtedness to him, rebuttals from *J.J.P.* and Cornwell continued to be based on one premise alone—that no one could give serious consideration to Chivers as a source of inspiration to Poe.

Writing under two pseudonyms "Fiat Justitia" and "Felix Forresti," Chivers was ready to give and to receive verbal assaults indefinitely; but there was a limit to the patience of Moses A. Dow, the *Waverly's* editor. He ended "Fiat Justitia's" outbursts with a published reprimand "We do not desire any more articles from him on that subject, or any other." In a letter to Chivers, Dow clearly indicated that he saw through his disguise. "I as willingly insert your articles as any other, if in a less nervous style; calling an opponent . . . 'dunderhead' . . . is no argument."[14] Although a few more articles in opposition to Chivers appeared in the *Waverly*, Dow for all practical purposes had withdrawn his journal from the fray.

Much of the argument revolves around similarity in meter and in the use of certain refrains. Chivers' protestations can be discounted and attributed to the frustration of a poet who smarted at public indifference to his work. Yet the problem can not easily be dismissed. One of the key issues is the use of the repetend "Nevermore" so familiar to readers of "The Raven." A similar refrain was definitely used by Chivers prior to the publication of Poe's poem in 1845. Among the Chivers' manuscripts at Duke University Library is a

poem dated July 20, 1828, Lexington, one stanza of which shows
relevance to the problem at hand:

> When shall we three here meet again,
> In love's familiar tone?
> When shall we three here meet again,
> In friendship all our own
> A voice then answered faint and low,
> From yon far-distant shore;
> Whose name I sought at once to know—
> Said he to me—'No more!'[15]

Entitled appropriately "No More!" the above poem might possibly
have been published in one of the countless magazines or newspapers
going in and out of business daily in those times. Chivers usually tried
to get his poems into print. A poem composed in 1828, seventeen
years prior to the publication of "The Raven" in 1845, had good
chances of being accepted by some magazine or newspaper long
before that.

"No More" provides some evidence that Chivers was in a certain
sense correct in claiming he had first used the basic theme, pattern,
and refrain of "The Raven" with its haunting imagery and echo. If "No
More" remained unpublished, it might have been one of the poems
sent by Chivers to the *Southern Literary Messenger* that Poe recalled
having seen in the 1830's. Out of respect for Poe Chivers apparently
said nothing about the similarity between "No More" and "The
Raven" before Poe's death. In the furor raging over his alleged theft of
material from Poe, the excitable Chivers must have completely
forgotten a poem in his files which might have won him some
additional support. Even then many commentators today would
claim that a comparison between "No More" and "The Raven" is
unconvincing; they would attribute any resemblance to a generally
shared literary style and translation of subject matter and theme,
rather than to plagiarism or borrowing. To be sure, Chivers' title
phrase "No More," is not comparable to "Nevermore" as used by Poe
within a poetic context of greater complexity and power. Further-
more, Chivers himself plays the copycat in openly taking a familiar
line from *Macbeth* and adapting it to his own poem which he writes
"When shall we three here meet again. . ."

Despite the above arguments, the existence of the manuscript of
"No More" may help at least to clarify Chivers' insistence on his own
originality. It would explain his reaction to the charge that "Isadore"

in *Eonchs of Ruby* (1851) with the line, "Back to Hell, thou ghostly Horror!" is little more than a clever paraphrase of "The Raven." To Chivers' way of thinking "Isadore" might have been a paraphrase, instead, of his own work, since Chivers intended "Isadore" as a tribute to Poe. There is also reason to believe "Isadore" was composed prior to 1845 when "The Raven" first appeared. In a letter to Poe, February 21, 1847 Chivers quotes three lines from "Isadore" and alludes to them as a passage with which Poe should be thoroughly familiar.[16] Whether or not Poe borrowed from an early version of "Isadore" remains of course highly speculative at best.

To cite another example of Poe's indebtedness, a selection from *The Lost Pleiad* (1845) brings to mind another of Poe's well-known poems, "The Bells":

> The funeral bell keeps tolling, keeps tolling,
> Keeps tolling for the dead;
> Whose azure sound goes rolling, goes rolling
> Like water, o'er my head![17]

The poem, "The Mother's Lament on the Death of Her Child," written August 10, 1841; provides adequate grounds for Chivers to point an accusing finger at the author of "The Bells." On the other hand, Chivers was not above imitating "The Bells" in "Requiem on the Death of Henry Clay."

Damon, besides supporting Chivers' contention that Poe took the format of "The Raven" from him, sees a strong resemblance between "Nacoochee" and "Ulalume." Poe acquired from Chivers, Damen suggests, certain ideas, such as the notion of the poet's mourning the loss of an ideal woman symbolic of the soul and of the contrast of chastity with passion; in both poems Death intervenes to snatch away the spotless virgin.[18]

Other examples could be cited, but suffice it to say that both Chivers and Poe owed much to each other, for theirs was a mutual debt unmarred by any furtive attempt at literary theft. The mid-nineteenth century, despite its Puritanical statements about plagiarism, had paradoxically an easygoing outlook on what constituted common literary property. Chivers borrowed, as Watts and Damon noted,[19] ideas and themes from other poets, a common practice at the time. It was also the period when, without an international law on copyright, foreign works were translated and published in America with no worry about payment of royalties.

To the end, the Georgian poet expostulated about Poe's debt to him and how his own poetic inspiration came in the form of "revelations of an equal blending of passion with fortuitous art." Although Poe possessed "manifestations of art in its highest forms," it was devoid of the supernatural light enjoyed by Chivers. By September, 1854, only the *Georgia Citizen* would print Chivers' arguments against Poe. Readers today would take exception to the charge "The Raven" had "paucity of rhyme" and find many of Chivers' points a bit exaggerated. One statement in the *Georgian Citizen* places in sharp relief the Georgian's undeniable originality as an esthetic theorist who envisioned a poem as "a melodious whole" designed to produce for "the ear precisely the same musical pleasure that is occasioned in the mind by its rhythmical articulation."[20] Observations such as this and the possibilities for growth Chivers saw in poetry represent the originality and foresight for which he is remembered today. Far less significant is the controversy over Poe even though Chivers fought tooth and nail on every issue as though his literary fame depended on it.

CHAPTER 10

Chivers and the Georgian Folk Tradition

I *Background*

SOME of the objections Eastern critics had against Chivers may be traceable in part to the interest he took in the folklore of his own region as expressed in the customs, music, and tales which echoed the spirit of the common people of Georgia. The extent to which music played a part in the life of the average Georgian is colorfully depicted in an anecdote in A. B. Longstreet's *Georgia Scenes* about a native son who, after a long absence out East, returns home to participate once more in a square dance: ". . . Off went the party to a good old republican six reel. I had been thrown among *fashionables* so long that I had almost forgotten my native dance. But it revived rapidly as they wheeled through its mazes, and with it returned many long-forgotten pleasing recollections. Not only did the reel return to me, but the very persons who used to figure in it with me, in the heyday of youth."[1]

The pangs of nostalgia felt by the gentleman endeavoring to recall a step he could dance easily in his youth were also experienced by Chivers throughout his career as a writer. He enjoyed the cultural opportunities in the East but also recognized that the Southern heritage had its value. Many of his poems recall the popular tunes and church hymns so important to residents of the South. Longstreet underscores this very fact in a portrait of one Georgian in a pew on Sunday morn: "This being the Sabbath, at the usual hour Ned went to church, and selected for his morning service one of those churches in which the pews are free, and in which the hymn is given out, and sung by the congregation . . . . As soon as the tune was raised, Ned struck in, with one of the loudest, hoarsest, and most discordant voices that ever annoyed a solemn assembly."[2] Chivers must have sung with equal vigor, and far greater religious fervor and commitment than Ned. An early Baptist up-

108

bringing brought Chivers into contact with church music and hymn singing. Since Chivers' family was in moderately comfortable circumstances without being Virginian Cavaliers, it had closer contact with the people. Besides, the genteel classes in Virginia were usually Anglicans or Presbyterians. Georgia, still in the process of emerging from the frontier stage of its history, represented by comparison a rougher and more homespun society.

II *Hymns and Folk Songs*

The faith Chivers knew was a folk religion removed from urban influences. Among Baptists and Methodists, zeal could easily reach the heights of hysteria. Even when this unbridled fervor was toned down, the basic emotionalism and the simple, unelaborate theology could be discerned in the hymnals. The primary message was the immediate communion of man's soul with the Redeemer; an organized church and clergy were of secondary importance. With this sense of freedom from dogma there came a desire to liberate church singing from the stiff confines of lifeless, composed scores. Instead, folk tunes, largely of Scottish and English origin, were used and the words changed or adapted to fit the popular taste of the rugged members of a Baptist congregation. A reading of these early hymn books discloses a large number of secular tunes based on patriotic and pastoral themes in the same volume with sacred songs. Before the advent of the hymn book, Georgia had an oral tradition that flourished among Baptists and Methodists providing a ready source for church and secular music.[3]

By the 1830's and 40's, song manuals were available that assured a permanent record of the rich oral tradition already in existence. The first edition of William Walker's *Southern Harmony* was published in 1835; the lines of two selections in it are worth quoting. "Long Time Ago" is a moving reminder of the Crucifixion:

> Jesus died on Calvary's mountain
>   Long time ago.
> And salvation's rolling fountain,
>   Now freely flows
> Once his voice in tones of pity,
>   Melted in wo,
> And he wept o'er Judah's city,
>   Long time ago.[4]

Another hymn, written by William Walker himself, "An Address for All," firmly cautions Southern whites to remember that on Judgment Day all members of society will be in the same straits:

> The princes high and beggars die, and mingle with the dust,
> The rich, the brave, the negro slave, the wicked and the just!
> Therefore prepare to meet thy God, before it be too late,
> Or else you'll weep, lament and cry, lost in a ruin'd state.[5]

One effect on Chivers of this mildly egalitarian statement is seen in a kind treatment of his own slaves. Suffice it to say, the hymnals used in Baptist churches opened the young Chivers' mind to various facets related to everyday living in Georgia. Other hymns and songs could be quoted that warn the sinner of impending damnation or relate the innocent joys of a summer night of singing on the back porch. Mention should be made too of the prefaces to some of the hymnals in use and their remarks on the function of music which may have affected Chivers. *Southern Harmony* has an introduction, taken from William Moore's *Columbian Harmony* (1825), that gives high priority to music in the divine scheme: ". . . It had its origin in God, and from God it was communicated to angels and men. Long before this world's foundations were laid, angels and archangels sang their grateful praises to the eternal Jehovah, encircling his throne and infinitely exulting. . . ."[6]

Collections that record the earlier oral tradition in sacred music, *Missouri Harmony*, *Hesperian Harp*, and *Harp of Columbia*, echo the words of William Moore in their prefaces; they trace the origin of music to God who gave to mankind the harmony of the universe and the angelic choirs.[7] Some of these notions appear to have been adapted by Chivers to fit his individualistic and Swedenborgian esthetics. To a great extent they are commonplaces but, preceding on the justifiable premise that Chivers acquired many things from his early training, it is advisable to examine the sources immediately available to Chivers. While on the subject of Chivers' esthetics, one selection from *Harp of Columbia* is worthy of mention. It is a simple round in three parts:

> The bell doth toll, its echoes roll,
> I know the sound full well.
> Bomb, bomb, bim, bomb bell.
> I love its ringing, for it calls to singing,
> With its bim, bim, bim, bomb bell.[8]

Artless as the round may appear, the onomatopoetic pattern of this ditty, or a similar one, could have lingered in Chivers' memory and suggested to him the potentialities of sonic effects in poetry.

The mind of Chivers did not always dwell on religion. Current trends and events attracted his attention and he was in many ways a man of his time living and enjoying the present. Among the favorite subjects treated in folk tunes were many about infidelity resulting in physical violence and death. Murder ballads make up one of the important subgenres of folk music. Chivers wrote an occasional poem on this theme and based an entire play, *Conrad and Eudora,* on an actual event that became a Southern legend.

The poet was well acquainted with folk music. There are references in his writings to the basic instruments of the time, the dulcimer, the five string banjo, and the fiddle as well as to popular tunes and dancing.[9] In an article in the *Georgia Citizen,* he complained that Northerners had no appreciation of the South and even less understanding; the average person up North had little knowledge of Black dialect and singing. So-called minstrel shows were not only the butt of Chivers' ridicule but a sign also of his defensiveness when Southern folk culture came under fire.[10] Much as he was fascinated by the glitter and polish of the East, deep down in his heart Chivers suffered from the same homesickness as the Georgian described by Longstreet; too long a stay among the "fashionables" of New York and Boston only contributed further to the poet's nostalgia.

III   Death of the Devil

The Georgia Citizen published in successive issues of November 13, 20, and December 4, 1852, a farce by Chivers entitled *Death of the Devil, A Serio-Ludrico, Tragico-Comico, Nigero-Whiteman Extravaganza.* The comedy was written for presentation "in two very remarkable side-cracking and soul-dissolving acts," and a "dark corner" of Lincoln, a town in Georgia, provided the locale of the action which begins with a white person, James, accusing Lee, a Black slave, of stealing a "gobler."[11]

Additional complications arise in other parts of Lincoln when Sally Jones tells Bill Barlow, the fiddler, that they can not be married because of Maw Jones' objections; the extent of the mother's animosity is displayed when she chases Bill off her property.

At the start of the second act James once more thrashes Pete in front of the other slaves for turkey stealing and the enraged Black

swears to even the score with James. As for Billy Barlow, he is
disconsolate about his inability to wed Sally Jones and finds solace in
playing his fiddle. He wishes he had the money to wed Sally, but tells
his mother he has no desire to work at the mill bequeathed to him by
his father.

Other members of Lincoln society put aside their financial problems and turn to lighter topics of conversation. Mrs. Cunningham
and Mrs. Dudley joke about the chronic pain in Mrs. Jumble's
stomach. When Mrs. Jumbles leaves home for a while the slaves sing
joyfully.

> Her husband raise her out ob de ashes
> He ought to gib he a tousan lashes
> Behase she hab her spasms dayly
> An'squall aloud for her Mabala
> Get out ob de way, yoo nasty yaller
> Yore powdered face is like ole taller.[12]

Unaware of the slaves' ridicule, Mrs. Jumble complains to Mr.
Jumble of continued abdominal pains. The doctor, on being sum-
moned, finds nothing wrong with Mrs. Jumble except her constant
grumbling. An interesting sidelight of this scene is the fact that,
although Mr. Jumble speaks the language of a Southern white, his
wife replies in Black dialect. This dialect explains why the Blacks in
their song referred to her as a "nasty yaller," a light-skinned member
of their own race married to a white farmer.

Jesse returns the money he had stolen to Mrs. Jones, and regrets
that he killed his friend Billy, whom he did not recognize disguised in
a devil costume. As for Mrs. Jones' offer of Sally's hand, Jesse declines
because "She stands entirely too high in this world for me"; he advises
the girl to marry a lawyer or doctor.[13]

Of chief importance in the rambling and disconnected farce are
Chivers' insights into local color, especially Black folklore and music.
Pete and Berry in the midst of their arguing about religion break into
a song:

> I'm gwine away to Allerbama
>   Long time ago!
> Den away to Tawscaloosa
> I cross de big Oogee Ribber
>   Long time ago!

> Now I feel my heart is brakin'
>   Long time ago!
> Dass to see you awl so sorry
>   Long time ago!
> Ip I never moare shell see you
>   Long time ago!
> We shell meet in Hebin foreber—
>   Long time ago![14]

Life at best was uncertain for Black people. Living in bondage, families and friends could be abruptly separated when sold to different owners. Amidst the farce, *Death of the Devil*, the song "Long time ago," adapted from the Southern white folk tradition, conveys the somber yet hopeful message that, despite separation on earth, reunion will take place in a better world.

The farce itself is inconsequential and obviously patterned after minstrel shows with the usual breaks for spontaneous singing. In this connection, Chivers shows considerable acquaintance with Black songs and those of the Georgia yeomen. Billy Barlow, the fiddler, alludes to a tune "Sally in the Wilderness" which was undoubtedly one of many pieces popular at square dances. In addition, Chivers pokes fun at the foibles of both white farmers and their slaves and their superstitions. In a better educated society, a devil's outfit would not be taken so seriously.

Beneath the banter and vulgarity of the society described in *Death of the Devil* is the grim reminder of the presence of social evils and inequality. In real life the thrashings received by the bewildered Pete were a brutal form of punishment. Mrs. Jumble, the "yaller" wife, represents the fate of many comely quadroons who became the object of a slaveholder's lust. The one encouraging note is the evidence that Chivers did not seem to approve of these abuses, especially the whipping of slaves. Otherwise he would not have included the song in which the Blacks taunt Mrs. Jumble nor would he have made mention of Pete's urge to take revenge on James who used the whip too freely. The means Pete employed to avenge himself, while comical and understandable within the context of the play, show, nonetheless, that prior to the Civil War Blacks were aware of insults to their manhood.

Despite certain drawbacks, the *Death of the Devil* reveals a realism in dialogue and local color definitely lacking in Chivers' other plays with the exception of *Conrad and Eudora*. It is perhaps somewhat ironic that, towards the end of his writing career, Chivers treated a subject very familiar to him: the people of his own native Georgia. Had he developed this interest earlier, he might have achieved some degree of fame in his lifetime.

IV *Chivers' Attitude towards the Blacks*

Being a slaveholder Chivers felt obliged to defend the cruel institution of human bondage against the attacks of Northern Abolitionists. As already seen in the *Death of the Devil,* he displayed some sympathy for slaves abused by their masters; but a little known poem in the Chivers collection at Duke University throws additional light on the poet's views about Black-white relationships. The following poem, entitled "The Silent Voice," is dated 1837:

> The stripes that on their backs were laid
> Shall heal before their eyes;
> And they shall see their servants made
> Their masters in the skies.
> That here the sweat oozed from his brow,
> Beneath the lash's smart,
> Hell's colter shall deep furrows plough
> In his damned Master's heart![15]

"The Silent Voice" furnishes welcome evidence that at an early date Chivers had enlightened views for a Georgian reared on a plantation where slave help was taken for granted. Most likely his father had treated slaves kindly and had set a good example for his son. Chivers' correspondence indicates that he himself looked after the welfare of his charges and made sure they were properly fed.[16] Such paternalism was the height of magnanimity at the time when Chivers saw the brutality practiced by many overseers. Specific laws designed to protect slaves were not only scarce but rarely enforced. Few slaveholders who maltreated Blacks were ever found guilty in the courts. Once, a jury in Georgia did agree that a master was guilty of manslaughter in whipping a slave to death but the culprit was released. Many Blacks had horrible scars from severe lashings or from torture by hot irons. Such bestial treatment led to frequent attempts to escape and occasional revolts.[17]

Chivers, in spite of his habitual irascibility, was at bottom kind-hearted and disapproved of the cruel handling of Blacks. Defense of slavery as an institution was for him a matter of upholding a social structure essential to Southern economy but Chivers did not allow this position to justify the wholesale abuse and torture of unfortunate human beings. His religious instincts obliged him to admit that the master had a certain reponsibility to watch over slaves in his care. The Georgian writer, like most Southerners, considered them oversized children totally dependent on white society for their livelihood. This attitude is not surprising in light of the estimate that, prior to the Civil War, only 5,000 out of 400,000 slaves in Georgia could read and write.[18]

Under such circumstances, the Black had few outlets to voice his frustration. The most despondent ones often chose suicide, but the majority of slaves voiced their misery in song. While their music was outwardly mirthful and lighthearted, it was merely a coverup for the despair produced by their bondage. The movement of Black songs was lively and rapid, a reflection of everyday work in the fields. Secular songs conceived of time as past events, but in hymns time signified the future in the day of judgment. Strongly aware of his own ego, the Black in his singing focussed attention on himself, on other persons, or on things related to his condition. For this reason, the lyrics often concern the singer and fellow slaves, or some physical point of reference whether a river or an animal. The basic syntax would often consist of conditional clauses which picture what might have happened if things were otherwise.[19]

Repetition of lines and refrains with skillful variation characterized the usual ditty sung or chanted by slaves. Rhyme and rhythm went hand in hand, and both served as convenient mnemonic devices in helping singers recall a particular song. Often the meaning would be subordinated to rhyme, rhythm, and harmony. In other words, the successful and pleasing production of a captivating pattern of sound was more important than the communication of a precise message. The evocation of certain moods or emotional states would naturally be better suited to a people with no immediate tradition of a formalized culture.[20]

In the composition of rhymes the Blacks took considerable liberty. Final consonants were usually dropped especially at the end of a rhyme. The use of meter was equally informal. Short lines were coordinated with long ones and long words were scanned exactly as the same as shorter ones. With such flexible prosody a versatile composer could hit upon unusual effects and combinations. Not every metric system allows two syllables to be counted as one. The omission of pronouns and conjunctions gave additional liberty to a free and easy tunesmith. There was considerable latitude in the variations of word pronunciation so a composer could produce subtle harmonies with few strained rhymes or dissonant sounds. Another pleasant feature of Black folk verse was that it usually fitted measures of music in 4/4 or 2/4 time.[21]

The natural gift the Blacks possessed for rhythm and melody is substantiated by their contribution to American music. This talent came in handy with the hard conditions of labor to which they were subjected. Undoubtedly work songs broke the monotony of their toil. The results were probably best in large gangs of men employed in the fields or in the construction of roads or buildings. It was a partial antidote to a life of painful drudgery.[22]

From his early days in Georgia Chivers heard slaves singing. Evidence that he took the subject of Black music seriously may be read in his criticism of G. P. Morris' "On the lake where drooped the willow" which the Georgian traces to a "nigger origin" because of Morris' use of the refrain "Long time ago." Chivers knew very well the same refrain was found in white folk tunes but had at the moment a bone to pick with Morris and Northerners in general for their ignorance of authentic Black music. Many people in the North, he wagered, had never heard slaves singing and working in the fields. Morris in particular would probably be startled to hear a real Black sing; minstrel shows, written by Northerners, were despised by Chivers who wrote *"Death of the Devil"* to counteract spurious versions by outsiders. "Susannah don't you cry!" was to the Georgian an especially revolting example of a distortion of authentic Black tunes. To set the record straight he provided a version of a work chant:[23]

> Jinny had de black eye
> Jinny was de gal!
> Git away de cawn boys!
> Git away de cawn! (Repeat)[24]

Blacks themselves, insisted Chivers, resented Northern indifference to their folk customs. While in the East, he on one occasion witnessed a Black whose singing in the street was ridiculed by a group of Northerners. After threatening his taunters with God's justice, he went off continuing his song. "Meat upon de goose feet, An' marrow in de boane!"

Ignorance of Black language was characteristic of most Northerners in the opinion of Chivers, who cited Harriet Beecher Stowe's *Uncle Tom's Cabin* as an atrocious example of an Abolitionist's total misconception of the fundamentals of Black speech. By way of example, Chivers presented a pun in Black language to the effect that General Scott's pen was like a "ribber in Maine," namely, "Pen-ob-Scot."[26]

To remedy the deplorable situation resulting from the absence of any serious study of Black music and from Northern misinterpretations and distortions, Chivers proposed that the task be undertaken by some learned Southerner. Corn-shucking songs and others of a similar nature were fit subjects for such a research project he suggested. Judging from Chivers' ability to record rather accurately Black songs and to capture their forceful, almost hypnotic rhythm, the Georgian himself was well qualified to edit such an anthology. The "Corn-Shucking Song," composed in 1853 in Massachusetts and published in the South two years later in the *Georgia Citizen*, demonstrates Chivers' feeling for the energy and vigor of Black work songs:

> Jinny boke de hoecake, Sally make de cawphy,
> Nancy bile de bakyon wid de brack-ey pea;
> Cuffy blow de Ram's Hawn, Juba beat de banjo—
> Dinah ring de Tin Pan to cawl us awl to Tea.
> Pull away, Niggers! oh! pull away, Darkies!
> De Bakyon's in de washpot, de bred upon de hoe,
> Shuck de Cawn, Darkies! oh! shuck de Cawn, Niggers!
> De Mawnin' Stars a-risin; de Sebin Stars are low!
> Git away de Cawn, Boys! git away de Cawn!
> Oh! git away de Cawn, Boys! git away de Cawn!
> Linkydum-a-hyadum, a-linkydum-a-ho!
> Beller, Boys! beller! de Cawn is gettin low![27]

Not inclined to be modest about his accomplishments, Chivers boasted of his familiarity with "Ethiopian" melodies which he maintained had more spontaneity than the "Caucasian."

From a comparative study of white and Black music, anyone could acquire a "better knowledge of the physiology as well as psychology of the two nations than can be found either in tradition or History."[28] As proof, Chivers quoted a song with the refrain "Too Mark-a-Juba!" and then drew the following conclusion; "There is no such rhythm as this in the Greek poetry—nor, in fact, in any other Nation under the sun. There is no dance in the world like that of Juba—the name of that . . .

provoking jig which accompanies this recitative—the very climax of jocularity—being as far above the Pyrrhic as the Tarantula in provoking laughter accompanied by irresistible shouts of uproarious hilarity."[29]

The above statement leaves little doubt concerning not only Chivers' interest in Black folk art but also his conviction that popular melody and rhythm had something to contribute to conventional art forms. Seldom was he so outspoken in his regionalism—although the underlying influence of the home country can be detected in his writings. A sketch from his papers shows his contact with the Black people working for him; it is a drawing of a slave stripped to the waist with his tongue hanging out, as though panting heavily, and his right hand is pointing out some object. The caption underneath reads, "Pete tellin' whar de diggs is."[30]

Basing his conviction on a close acquaintance with Black culture, Chivers firmly maintained that here was "absolutely more real and soul thrilling music made audible . . . by the impassioned utterance of the Negroes in the South . . . than can be found . . . in these whole Northern regions." He repeated this argument when submitting "De Ole Gray Hoss" to the editor of the *Knickerbocker:* "You can never know how really exquisite they are until you hear the music to which they are indissolubly united." As for the authenticity of "De Ole Gray Hoss," Chivers guaranteed the poem was a faithful transcription of the lines "originally composed by the Ethiopian improvisatore." The down-to-earth humor of the text testifies to the conscientious effort on Chivers' part to preserve the purity of the original:[31]

> I wen down to de ribber,
> An' I coodn't git across,
> An I gib fifty cents
> Fur an' ole gray hoss
> De ole gray hoss he mired in de san;
> An de way dis nigger did grabble fur de lan'!
> Oh! whar did yoo kum fum,
> Kum fum, kum fum
> To knock a nigger down?[32]

Chivers noted the Black's seemingly jovial acceptance of his burden, an impression many outsiders mistakenly received when scanning the text of work songs. The Georgian poet was able to penetrate that deceptive facade of amiability to discover an abiding faith in immortality and in the prospect of a better life that motivated the slaves to survive. "Ole Georgy Joe," a whimsical piece, sums up the sober reflections of one Black on his lot. Pride in his virility and hope of an eternal reward sustain him in his resignation as he strives to impart this feeling to an older friend:

> Doane yoo heer dis Niggur hollur,
> Old Georgy Joe?
> Sowner dan a silbur dollur.
> Ole Georgy Joe?
> . . . .
> May de Chay-yot of Alyjur
> Ole Georgy Joe!
> Kum fum Heben abobe to blidge yoo,
> Ole Georgy Joe![33]

Jay Hubbell, who had definite reservations about Chivers' rank among American poets, did not hesitate to acknowledge the Georgian's ability to grasp the rhythm and soul of Black language and music.[34] This recognition is significant since, in the nineteenth century, only a few writers before Joel Chandler Harris tried to reproduce Black language with any degree of accuracy. It was conventional to resort to misspelling when recording Black speech to convey an adequate concept of its distinctive intonation and patterns. Under the circumstances Chivers was a more faithful recorder than his contemporaries. Over twenty years before Harriet Beecher Stowe's novel was published, he was already transcribing the speech and the music of the slaves.

Hubbell's dislike of misspelling as a means of registering the sound patterns of Black folk verse does not seem an adequate argument in view of the need for an accurate phonetic transcription. Deeply aware of and sensitive to shadings of pitch and tone, Chivers could be trusted to reproduce conscientiously the lyrics of the Black tunes he heard. His renditions conform in the main with the principles of Black meter, rhyme, and rhythm. At this point, the question might well be raised concerning the extent to which Chivers, in composing his own poems, was influenced by slave songs. The same possibility has been raised in regard to Poe who lacked Chivers' interest in Black music and dialect.

The extent to which Chivers appreciated Black folk verse and music may be ascertained from his belief that formal learning and culture were not the only sources of artistic inspiration; "It is the belief of man . . . that the School books enumerate all the rhythms in which any poem can be written. But the truth is, by ingenious combination, infinite numbers can be produced . . . I have long thought that I could write a paper on the various rhythms of the Ethiopians compared with those now in use of the Caucasian race. . . ."[35]

The implication is clear. Chivers believed that the folk songs and music of Georgian Blacks, as well as whites, had something to offer the poet. With his frequent emphasis on the pristine quality of writers in the early period of man's history, he logically would draw upon sources in his own immediate social milieu which, in his estimation, retained the spontaneity and enthusiasm of the composers of lyrics in simpler and less inhibited societies. The folk heritage of his native region then was understandably irresistible in its attraction to Chivers.

V Chivers' Poetic Devices

The singular effects attained in many of Chivers' poems can be attributed to his preoccupation with producing in poetry a variety of sounds. He accomplished his objective through onomatopoeia even to the point of inventing words when necessary. Rhythm was also extremely important to him. (It has already been noted how impressed he was by the rhythmic patterns of Black songs.) From the very first, he took much interest in the form and structure of his poems and experimented with a nine-line stanza, a-b-a-b-c-d-c-d-d, Spenserians, and blank verse. In Nacoochee, Chivers used the refrain, couplets, and the rhyme schemes a-b-a-b and a-a-a-b-b-b. In the sonnet he tried several variations in the Lost Pleiad, which has some good attempts although they reveal little or no awareness of the intricacies of the sonnet. Eonchs of Ruby, Virginalia and Atlanta contain poems written for the sake of hypnotizing the auditor or reader and impressing him with the melodic pattern.

Chivers never liked to use a standard poetic form without altering it. He discarded the blank verse after trying it a short period in the 1830's. The quatrain was one of his favorites—but even then he had to alternate trimeter, tetrameter, and pentameter lines to satisfy his urge to experiment. Often his stanzas would vary from three to eleven lines in length.

An inappropriate choice of words frequently led to needless bungling on Chivers' part especially in his a-b-a-b-c-d-c-d-d variation of the Spenserian. Possibly the best results with this form are obtained in "Apollo":

> Like some deep, impetuous river from the fountains everlasting,
> Down the serpentine soft valley of the vistas of all Time,
> Over cataracts of adamant uplifted into mountains
> Soared his soul to God in thunder on the wings of thought sublime,
> With the rising golden glory of the sun in ministrations,
> Making oceans metropolitan of splendor for the dawn—
> Piling pyramid on pyramid of music for the nations—
> Sings the Angel who sits shining everlasting in the sun,
> For the stars, which are the echoes of the shining of the sun.[36]

This nine-line stanza, unlike less successful attempts in this form, has a unity of effect and impression that Chivers did not always attain. The repetition in the last two lines is forceful, and the reader does not have the feeling that additional unrelated lines were added merely to have the required number in a stanza.

Blank verse was a stumbling block for Chivers in *The Path of Sorrow* (1832), and his experiments with it were indeed primitive; this first volume does reveal his embryonic interest in the mechanics of poetry. The refrain is not found in *The Path of Sorrow*, but by 1853 *Virginalia* has scarcely a poem without one. This poetic device was a logical choice for Chivers, bent on expanding the function of rhythm and sound in poetry. His fondness for folk ballads sensitized him to the autosuggestive potentialities of the skillful handling of repetends. One of the best examples perhaps is "Avalon" where the repetitive strains convey to the reader the auditory and visual sensations of a woodland scene:

> Thy soul did soar up to the Gates of God,
>   Oh, Lark-like Child!
> And poured Heaven's Bowers of Bliss, by Angels trod,
>   Poured Wood-notes wild!
> In emulation of that Bird, which stood
> In solemn silence, listening to thy flood
> Of golden melody deluging the wood
>   Where thou are lying
>   Beside the beautiful undying

> In the Valley of the Pausing of the Moon,
> Oh! Avalon! my son! my son![37]

Sometimes Chivers utilizes the refrain as a prefatory declaration. The poet handles this device rather deftly in "The Dying Beauty" in which he graphically portrays the death of a fair lady:

> She died in beauty, like the morn that rose
> In golden glory on the brow of night,
> And passed off gently like the evening's close,
> When days last steps upon the heavens are bright.
> She died in beauty, like the trampled flower
> That yields its fragrance to the passer's feet,
> For all her life was as an April shower
> That kept the tear-drops of her parting sweet.[38]

The foregoing lines are rendered more firm and compact by the introductory refrain, "She died in beauty." In this instance, Chivers' inventive impulses produced fairly substantial dividends.

Reared in the South where oratory was glorified as a manly art of expressing patriotism and the triumph of liberty over tyranny, Chivers was affected by this trend from the onset of his literary career. The melodrama, *Conrad and Eudora*, furnishes early evidence of his desire to compose declamatory verse. Subsequently he developed this mode of expression in patriotic lyrics. One of the most noteworthy examples is "The Roll of Fame" in which Chivers' favorite a-b-a-b quatrain is used forcefully but with rather rough octameters. The even number lines are catalectic:

> In the Autumn of the world, when the honey of the
> Summer still lay on the flowers of the years,
> I stood on the evergreen banks of the
> beautiful River of Time,
> And there I heard the loud thunders, rolled off
> from the prows of the crystalline Spheres,
> Break calmly against the white shore of my
> panting soul in utterance sublime.[39]

Whatever drawbacks "The Roll of Fame" might have in unevenness of composition are more than compensated for by the overall cadence and improvement of its lines. The reader can sense some of the emotions experienced by Chivers in his spiritualistic vision of the cosmos.

Closely related to Chivers' experiments with meter and refrains was his desire to coin new terms and phrases to provide the sound effects he wished to create in poetry. Among his early neologisms are *smile-beams, zephyr-dimpled lake, island-clouds* and *shell-tones.* He could also invent exotic names like *Boscobella.* Some of these Chiversian words that appear in "The Soaring Swan" conjure up images of hues and colors:

> For there shall flow
> From out the circlings of thy floating form,
> Bathed in the flickering dalliance of the gems
> of thy sun-cinctured dimples, like the pearl
> Of ocean set in beryl by the deep—
> A shell-toned music . . . . .[40]

Among the poems in *Eonchs of Ruby* and *Virginalia* some, like "The Lusiad", rely almost entirely on the jolting sensation accomplished by the use of unusual sounding words:

> In the mild month of October
> As we did go
> Through the fields of Cooly Rauber,
> No one can know,
> But the great Archangel Auber,
> What songs did flow . . . .[41]

The literal meaning of the words at this point were of secondary consideration to Chivers who more and more focussed his attention on the connotations of the terms he employed. While he considered his peculiar system of poetics unique, he had no awareness of the far-reaching implications of tampering with the literal meaning of words.

In Chivers' imagination, color and sound became one, and the same sensation was readily interchangeable since identical terms could be used to describe both sensory reactions. His word portrait in "The Angelus" illustrates his clever application of this principle:

> A wave-like, azure sound,
> Upon the pavement of new-fallen snow

> Pure as an Angel's garment upon the ground—
> Trembling the atmosphere with its soft flow—
> Comes swiftly, with its Heaven-dialating swell,
> From the Noon-ringing of yon far-off Bell. [42]

Chivers' study of color and its sonic connotations prompted him to examine the artistic potentialities of a stronger stress on onomatopoeia with a corresponding deemphasis on the literal meaning of words. At the same time he realized even more the importance of alliteration and assonance. In Chivers' poems sound became more and more significant, and the idea contained in the poem, of less consideration. Because he was groping for a poetic form where the sonic factor was paramount, what resulted, at times, was an odd verbal magic. If the reader became completely unanalytical, he could allow himself to be ushered into a bizarre Chiversian world where an unconventional assortment of words conjured up startling but original images of sound and color. "The Little Boy Blue" builds up a cadence in its thirty-seven quatrains that produces that very effect:

> By the cool crystal rills,
> That meandered Lahawn,
> All along the green hills,
> There he wandered at dawn—
>
> From the forests of Dru,
> On the Mountains of Morn,
> Blowing songs ever new
> Through the throat of his horn. [43]

The overall impression of a maze of color and sound is accomplished in "The Little Boy Blue" by the arresting end-rhymes. Another poem must be read, however, to appreciate fully Chivers' determination to present a phonetic reproduction of bizarre sonic phenomena. "Chinese Serenade" records the sounds of a Chinese fretted instrument:

> Tien-Tsze
> Tu Du
> Skies Blue—
> All Clear—
> Fourth year,
> Third Moon,

> High Noon
> At night . . .

"Chinese Serenade" ends with a vigorous endeavor to imitate the striking of a gong: "Bo-an-owng, ba-ang bing! Bee-ee-eeing, ba-ang, bong!⁴⁵" Along with his experiments with the potential uses of sound in poetry, Chivers also realized that lines of poetry with a proper choice of onomatopoetic terms and end-rhymes could have a hypnotic effect on the reader. The "Railroad Song" vividly portrays through clever sonic manipulations a train pulling out of a station:

> All aboard! Yes—Tingle, tingle
> Goes the bell as we all mingle—
> No one sitting solely single—
> As the steam begins to fizzle
> With a kind of sighing sizzle
> Ending in a piercing whistle. . .⁴⁶

The a-a-a-b-b-b rhyme scheme and the close and cagey juxtaposition of similar sounds testify to Chivers' ability as a poetic craftsman. There was some basis for his frequent accusation that many contemporary poets had little or no comprehension of the function of sound in poetry and that they lacked the incentive to investigate its possibilities. Chivers had the necessary imagination and a sensitive ear capable of distinguishing differences in tone that enabled him to experiment with new poetic devices.

The Georgian's experimental impulses often resulted in a free and loose poetic structure, especially in the use of similes. Although he was probably moved to employ similes after reading Shelley, he lacked the English poet's finesse; but Chivers occasionally composed some unique lines built around similes that usually relied upon the word *like*. At times *as* and *so* were also utilized. A tribute to Poe, "Caelicola," furnishes one of the better examples of Chivers' use of the simile:

> Like that sweet bird of night,
> Startling the ebon silence from repose,
> Until the stars appear to burn more bright
> From its excessive gush of song which flows
> Like some impetuous river to the sea—
> So thou did'st flood the world with melody.
> For as the evening star

126   THOMAS HOLLEY CHIVERS

> Pants with its "silver lightnings" for the high
> And holy Heavens—the azure calm afar—
> Climbing with labor now the bending sky
> To lead Night's Navy through the upper sea—
> So thou did'st pant for immortality. [47]

One of Chivers' obsessions that in all probability was related to his Swedenborgianism in his inquiry into the mystical significance of silence. As a result of his probing into the sensations experienced in periods of silence, he chanced upon some arresting imagery in "The Retrospect":

> My chamber has become an alcove
> For the watchers of the sky! and in my
> Bed, at midnight of my sleep, I people
> Worlds, and dream unnumbered things; till silence
> Wakes from lethargy, and shocks my burning
> Brain . . . [48]

Mere intellectualization on the reader's part would be insufficient to penetrate the Chiversian world. The Georgian evidently expected the reader to have an active imagination similar to his where, in the imagery of the external physical world, he presented highly abstract levels of mystical and preternatural experience. The result was obviously a very vivid and immediate revelation for Chivers, judging from the haunting metaphor in the following lines from *"The Voice of the Exile":* "The last dark wave that lashed affection's shore, / Is pausing now upon my weary soul! / Thy syren mistress of its tides shall be / A lamp hung out beyond eternity!"[49]

In recording verbally his sensory perceptions Chivers was concerned not only with the visual and the auditory but also with the olfactory senses. The intermingling of various sensations constituted a sort of poetic exercise for Chivers, and he seemed to take delight in baffling and confusing the reader. In "The Voice of Thought," he endeavored to describe his mental and emotional states in a typical moment of inspiration when all sensory images assumed some vague semblance of unity in his feverish brain:

> Faint as the far-down tone
> Beneath the sounding sea,
> Muffled, by its own moan,
> To silent melody;

> So faint we cannot tell
> But that the sound we hear
> Is some sweet rose's smell
> That falls upon our ear. . .[50]

The evocative quality of his words was readily apparent to Chivers whether or not he always fully profited by his discovery. Even when resorting to a more conventional poetic device of personification in "The Wind," he still cannot resist the urge to use his own distinctive juxtaposition of words: "Thou wringest, with thy invisible hand, the foam / Out of the emerald drapery of the sea, / Beneath whose foldings lies the Sea-Nymph's home— / Lifted, to make it visible, by thee . . ."[51] The Chiversian touch is still discernible in a standard personification of the wind. Descriptions like "invisible hand" and "emerald drapery" are distinctive signs of Chivers' unique interpretation of the data supplied to a fertile imagination by his alert and keen senses. Behind the immediate imagery lies Chivers' correspondential link to a higher world of spiritual truths dimly adumbrated by the physical world below. It was the poet's function, Chivers always maintained, to select and express in poetry those words and images that gave to the reader some inkling of the heavenly truths above. The Georgian in the final analysis felt, that his role was essentially sacerdotal in performing what amounted to a religious ritual.

CHAPTER II

Chivers' Reputation at Home and Abroad

I Chivers and His Contemporaries

CHIVERS' failure to win any substantial degree of recognition in his lifetime among his peers is attributable in part to his sarcastic and biting replies to anyone who had the nerve to criticize him. William Carey Richards, editor of the *Southern Literary Gazette*, soon discovered he could not with impunity point out defects in Chivers' style when he found himself duly rebuked by Chivers in 1850 for "impudence, presumption, egotism, and ignorant platitude."[1]

With critics who had at least partial praise for his efforts, Chivers couched his objections in more moderate terms. Habitual grouchiness did not blind him to the importance of maintaining good relationships with some contemporaries, however small their number, who had at least a few favorable things to say about his poetry. He might take exception to casual observations by Poe, Simms, or Augustine Duganne that did not please him; but he never started a vendetta because he had more than enough feuds to carry on as it was. Besides critics of his writings Chivers waged verbal warfare with the Abolitionists—those "Autocrats of Agitation;" Whittier and Horace Greeley were the special targets of his attacks.[2]

While Chivers used some restraint in saying that Poe was indebted to him for innovative ideas in imagery and meter, he bluntly labeled Longfellow an outright copy cat. *Hiawatha* was unquestionably an imitation of "Celuta" and *Atlanta* from the standpoint of versification. The *Kalevala* had no influence whatsoever on *Hiawatha* whose author could consult American poets writing on the Indian for necessary details on meter and subject matters. In addition to the versification of *Hiawatha* Chivers seems to imply that Longfellow acquired from "Celuta" and *Atlanta* the

128

inspiration to compose a narrative poem on the American aborigines.[3] The Georgian's contention is justified to some extent since he was at the time one of the foremost exponents of poetry based on Indian themes.

Resentment at the snobbery of the Eastern literary establishment centered primarily in the New York writers; "the *Literati* of Gotham" were excoriated by Chivers for preferring "the face of the very devil himself" to the "Portrait of Edgar A. Poe."[4] Disgust with their attitude towards Poe was not the sole factor in motivating Chivers' intense dislike of the literati. Possibly he was snubbed at one of the *conversazioni* held weekly by Anne Lynch Botta, a prominent figure in the New York literary scene.[5] George Ripley received a tongue lashing as the "dullest of all mystics" for daring in a rather patronizing manner to call the title *Eonchs of Ruby* "something mystical." Ripley and his crowd were absolutely incapable of penetrating "the inner life of things."[6] Other members of the literati were also raked over the coals. Nathaniel P. Willis was accused of obscenity in his choice of subject matter and of an "airy fantasqueness in style devoid of any substance."[7] Similarly, Griswold, already on Chivers' black list for attacking Poe, and his friends were judged persons of little consequence. "Brindle-whiskers and his set" were at best "short-sighted mortals."[8]

Although limited vision and a lack of foresight may have hindered the judgment of many of Chivers' peers especially when they placed a low value on his literary achievements, a poetic experimenter like Chivers should have expected some adverse criticism. There were of course certain critics who refused to see any merit in the Chiversian style. Richards of *The Orion* callously tore to shreds the delightful "To Allegra Florence in Heaven." Where students today detect considerable charm, Richards perceived nothing more than a "sad jumble of snow-white clouds."[9]

Other commentators echoed Richards' sentiments, but there were also those more equitable in their judgment. Augustine Duganne may have satirized a "Georgic Chivers" unable "to soar to strike the highest chord,"[10] but he had different views about *Eonchs of Ruby*. "We might quote passages of rare beauty throughout the book—passages which despite the faults . . . are replete with the loveliest developments of the divine idea in the man's soul."[11]

A fellow Southerner, William G. Simms, who had both favorable and unfavorable comments on *The Lost Pleiad*, was inclined to frown on Chivers' prolonged period of mourning for his daughter.[12] While Simms failed to discern Chivers' strong points, he was still superior to the hack magazine editors who took great delight in scathing censure of any writer they deemed inconsequential.

II Chivers' Posthumous Reputation

After Chivers' death Bayard Taylor in the 1870's looked back fondly on passages from "Rosalie Lee" and "Apollo" whose imagery struck his fancy.[13] When in England Taylor shared his liking for Chivers with Swinburne. With the exception of Taylor and perhaps a few friends in Georgia who still remembered their native poet, Chivers quickly faded into oblivion. By 1899 Charles A. Dana briefly recalled that the Georgian was a "literary freak" of the 1840's and 50's.[14] James A. Harrison, in a study of Poe and Chivers, had little to say in the latter's favor and helped to establish Chivers' reputation as a second-rate figure and as a slavish imitator of Poe, an opinion largely supported today.[15]

In view of Chivers' limited reputation in his lifetime and the oblivion he suffered after death it is surprising to learn that a few poets in the first part of the twentieth century knew of him. Joyce Kilmer checked out Nacoochee from the Columbia University Library.[16] When Professor Damon, an admirer of Chivers, had the opportunity to attend a lecture and poetry reading by the fiery and rhetorical poet from Illinois, Vachel Lindsay, Damon at the close of Lindsay's presentation discreetly inquired whether the Illinois poet was acquainted with Chivers. In characteristically unpredictable fashion, Lindsay promptly recited from memory several poems by Chivers! On that occasion in fact, Lindsay was complaining in the lecture attended by Damon, of Americans' ignorance of their own poets.[17]

Some of the strident lines Lindsay wrote several decades after Chivers' death are prefigured in poems like the "Chinese Serenade for the Ut-Kam and Tong-Koo,"[18] already quoted in Chapter 10. Lindsay would have several points in common with Chivers. The Illinois poet was also a faithful church-goer, a temperance lecturer, and loyal to the region of his birth. In view of his acquaintance with Chivers Lindsay may have in some degree been affected by the Georgian's insistence on poetic musicality. Lindsay had his own distinct notions on the lyricism essential to poetry and chanted many of his poems during public readings. Another experiment in imitating the rough sounds of the material world is made in "The Railroad Song", a foretoken of Lindsay's strong rhythms:

> Clitta, clatta, clatta, clatter,
> Like the devil beating batter
> Down below in iron platter,
> Which subsides into a clanky,
> And a clinky, and a clanky.
> And a clinky, clanky, clanky,
> And a clanky, clinky, clanky;
> And the song that now I offer
> For Apollo's Golden Coffer—
> With the friendship that I proffer—
> Is for Riding on a Rail.[19]

These poems capturing the harsh noises of an impending industrial age may have attracted Lindsay's attention. They anticipate in a measure the free swinging style of some modern American poets who describe the loud and nerve racking sounds of a commercial and industrialized society. In this respect Chivers appears as a precursor of twentieth-century Realism.

Since Chivers' death only occasional interest has been shown in his poems. When S. Foster Damon in 1930 suggested that the Georgian merited a reevaluation .as an important writer of the nineteenth century who had some influence on Poe, Landon Bell ridiculed Damon. To Bell Chivers was too inferior a poet to have any effect on Poe.[20] Charles Henry Watts' thoughtful reappraisal of Chivers in 1956 is supportive of Damon's study, and it no doubt prompted some scholars to reassess the Georgian poet.[21] Jay B. Hubbell's casual mention of Chivers is probably a more reliable indication of the general opinion among specialists concerning Poe's cantankerous associate.[22] Since few take the time to give Chivers the serious analysis he deserves much still remains to be done.

III *Chivers' Reputation in England*

When Bayard Taylor visited England in the 1870's he was startled on one occasion to hear Swinburne say, "Oh, Chivers, Chivers, if you know Chivers, give me your hand." To Taylor's amazement, Swinburne recited from memory several poems by the Georgian. With "shouts of delight" the two poets then swapped bizarre Chiversian passages.[23] While Swinburne found Chivers amusing, there was a more serious reason for the English poet's interest. The first stanza of Swinburne's "Delores" recalls the Georgian's "Lily Adair;" and in addition, the latter's "Song to Isa Singing" also influenced the British writer.[24] When two of Swinburne's contemporaries, Dante Gabriel Rossetti and his brother, William, came into possession of a copy of *The Lost Pleiad*, they were both struck by its singularity. During Horace E. Scudder's visit to England he met Gabriel, who made him promise to obtain information about Chivers. Upon his return to America, Scudder questioned James Russell Lowell who dubbed the Georgian "the shell of Shelly" and James T. Fields to whom Chivers was a "bore."[25] This intelligence had little effect on the Rossetti brothers. Gabriel apparently made use of themes and imagery from the "Soaring Swan" and "The Vigil in Aiden," and William included three selections from *The Lost Pleiad* in his *American Poems*. Today Gabriel's copy of *Eonchs of Ruby* is at the University of North Carolina Library.[26]

Any acquaintance with Chivers on the part of British writers is unusual in view of the limited circulation of the Georgian's work in America and the absence of any known reviews of his poetry in English journals of the nineteenth century. The British Museum presently has copies of *Virginalia* and *Atlanta*, but at one time, according to rumor, it had the only complete set of Chivers' works in the world. It is entirely possible that some inquisitive book collector from England visited America, became intrigued with Chivers, purchased all his available works, and subsequently donated them to the British Museum. As late as 1903, Rudyard Kipling, without acknowledging his source, borrowed from "The Poet of Love" by Chivers in composing "The Flies," one of the poems in *Five Nations*.[27]

The influence of Chivers on the PreRaphaelites is in keeping with the unpredictability of Chivers' career and with the uniqueness of his literary views and techniques. Needless to say, he would have been flattered to learn that the Rossettis, Swinburne, and Kipling read his poetry and incorporated some of his themes and imagery in their own work.

IV *Chivers and the French Symbolists*

John Sullivan Dwight, the Boston music critic and editor, received on March 3, 1853, a letter in which Chivers complimented him for the statement that Wagner had emancipated the "Poet from that completely menial relation in which he has stood to the musician, merely furnishing the latter with some slight verbal text for the forms in which he chooses to compose."[28] The Georgian had instantly applauded a sentiment which summarized his own thinking on music and poetry; for, even more than Dwight, Chivers realized that poets had to recapture the essentials of their art that they had relinquished to the composers. Mallarmé and the French Symbolists were to discover in Wagner a sonority they wished to incorporate into their own verse. Although they went farther than Chivers in abandoning the literal meaning of words, inventing new terms, and taking liberties with syntax, their innovations to a great extent had been anticipated by the eccentric Georgian. The latter longed for the applause of bourgeois society, the very group that French Symbolists endeavored to scorn and shock; but, like them, he resented a flippant school of critics too obtuse to see the true value of his theories.

It is paradoxical that Chivers, a practitioner of the worst features of Romanticism, still was attracted to a new concept of poetry that was to have its flowering in France. At the time he wrote to Dwight, Baudelaire was eager to translate Poe; and, shortly after Chivers had died, Mallarmé started to look upon Poe as one of the principal sources of Symbolist inspiration. It is highly doubtful that French Symbolists had any knowledge whatsoever of Chivers, a fact that becomes ironic when the genesis of the Georgian's poetics is traced to Swedenborg. The Scandinavian mystic had been well known to the French literary world since the early days of Romanticism; even the novelist Balzac came under the spell of the *Arcana Coelestia*. Although Poe in principle rejected Swedenborg, his insistence on the indefiniteness of music and poetry and on the interrelation of the two art forms owed something to the Swedish seer's hypothesis of the essential unity of all forms of sensory perception.[29]

French writers perceived a kindred spirit in Poe since he furnished them with sharp precise observations on literary theory that applied to poetry. The Gallic temperament, unlike the British, demanded a process of reasoning and critical evaluation to justify any new trend in literature. By this same token, Chivers would have been welcomed as one of their own. With Mallarmé, he could hear a spiritual melody that required ears sensitized to divine music. Baudelaire could have appreciated Chivers' perception of an endless series of correspondential relationships between the material and the immaterial orders. Gérard de Nerval would have noted that in many ways Chivers' exploration of the dream world paralleled the probings into the realm of the subconscious seen in *Les Filles du Feu*. In general, along with the Symbolists, Chivers was endeavoring to penetrate the phenomena of external reality in order to enter an inner world where new truths could be found. To the French Symbolist, this inner world was in the main a highly sublimated esthetic ideal; to the Georgian, it was a definite revelation expounded in the writings of Swedenborg.

Notes and References

Chapter One

1. Readers are referred to S. Foster Damon, *Thomas Holley Chivers: Friend of Poe* (New York, 1930) and Charles Henry Watts, *Thomas Holley Chivers: His Literary Career and His Poetry* (Athens, 1956) for details on Chivers' life.

2. Useful background references to Georgia's history and culture are: Ulrich B. Phillips, *Life and Labor in the Old South* (Boston, 1929): Robert P. Brooks, *History of Georgia* (Boston, 1913); Jay B. Hubbell, *The South in American Literature* (Durham, 1954); Francis P. Gaines, *The Southern Plantation: A Study in the Development and the Accuracy of a Tradition* (New York, 1925); Edwin Harrison Cady, *The Gentlemen in America* (Syracuse, 1949).

3. Details on the problems arising from Chivers' first marriage are outlined in *The Correspondence of Thomas Holley Chivers*, ed. Emma Lester Chase and Lois Ferry Parks (Providence, Rhode Island; 1957), pp. 2-7.

4. *The Letters of Edgar Allan Poe*, ed. John Ward Ostrom, (Cambridge, 1948), II, 498-9.

5. *Ibid.*, I, 295-9.

6. *Correspondence of Chivers*, pp. 49, 55, 60.

7. *Ibid.*, p. 38.

8. *Chivers' Life of Poe*, ed. Richard Beale Davis, (New York, 1952), p. 11.

9. *Letters of Edgar Allan Poe*, II, 373.

10. *Correspondefce of Chivers*, p. 74.

11. *Letters of Edgar Allan Poe*, II, 528.

12. *Correspondence of Chivers*, pp. 69-70.

13. *Chivers' Life of Poe*, pp. 39-52.

14. *Correspondence of Chivers*, pp. 32-36.

Chapter Two

1. Howard Mumford Jones, *Ideas in America* (Cambridge, 1944), p. 291.

2. See my article "Chateaubriand's American Reception (1802-1870)," pp. 221-228 in *Proceedings of the Commemoration of the Bicentenary of the Birth of Chateaubriand* (Geneva, 1970).

3. *Ibid.*, p. 222.

4. See my article "American Attitude Towards the French Romantics," *Revue de littérature comparée* (July-December, 1965), pp. 358-71.

5. "Chateaubriand's American Reception," pp. 222-23.

6. See my article, "French Romanticism on the American Stage," *Revue de littérature comparée* (January, 1970), pp. 161-72.

7. Roy Harvey Pearce, *The Savages of America* (Baltimore, 1953), p. 211; Albert Keiser, *The Indian in American Literature* (New York, 1933), p. 152.

8. *The Works of Edgar Allan Poe,* ed. Edmund Clarence Stedman and George Edward Woodberry (Chicago, 1895), I, 24, 176-77.

9. "Chateaubriand," *The New Yorker,* (July 13, 1836), p. 289.

10. Joseph Holt Ingraham, *The Southwest* (New York, 1835), II, 16, 226-31.

11. *The Journals of Francis Parkman* (New York, 1948), I, 324; George Bancroft and Charles Botta, *History of the United States from the Discovery of the American Continent to the End of the Late War* (Edinburg, 1843), p. 330.

12. See my article "An Old New York Salon-French Style," *New York Historical Society Quarterly* (January, 1971), pp. 38-51.

13. See my forthcoming article, "Longfellow's *Hiawatha* and Chateaubriand's *Atala*" in *Studi Francesi.*

14. Samuel Longfellow, *Life of Henry Wadsworth Longfellow* (London, 1886-87), III, 45.

15. Two English translations of Chateaubriand available to Chivers were: *Atala: or, The Amours of two Indians, in the Wilds of America* (London, 1802); *The Natchez, an Indian Tale* (London, 1827).

16. "The Chickamauga Indian's Conversion," p. 138, from *Songs of the Heart.*

17. James Adair, *The History of the American Indians* (London, 1775), pp. 29-36.

18. William Bartram, *Observations on the Creek and Cherokee Indians* (Philadelphia, 1789), pp. 11-31.

19. See footnote 15 of this chapter.

20. James Mooney, *Myths of the Cherokees* (Washington, 1902), pp. 416-17.

21. Rev. George White, *Historical Collections of Georgia* (New York, 1854), pp. 486-87; Lucian Lamar Knight, *Georgia's Landmarks, Memorials and Legends* (Atlanta, Georgia, 1914), II, 1032-33.

22. Mooney, *Myths of the Cherokees,* pp. 437-38.

23. Stith Thompson, *Motif-Index of Folk-Literature* (Bloomington, 1957), IV, 430-33.

24. Sir Paul Harvey, *The Oxford Companion to English Literature* (London, 1932), p. 442.

25. Frederick Webb Hodge, *Handbook of American Indians North of Mexico* (New York, 1959), II, 931-32.

26. Elizabeth Tooker, ed., *Iroquois Culture, history, and pre-history, Proceedings of the New York State Museum and Science* (Albany, 1967); Marian Emily White, *Iroquois culture history in the Niagara frontier area of New York State* (Ann Arbor, 1961).

27. Hodge, *Handbook of American Indians*, II, 874.

28. See Samuel G. Drake, *Chronicles of the Indians of America, from Its First Discovery to the Present Time* (Boston, 1836).

29. Mooney, *Myths of the Cherokees*, p. 321.

30. James Mooney, "The Cherokee River Cult," *Journal of American Folklore* (January-March, 1900), XIII, 1-10.

31. "To Readers and Correspondents," *New York Mirror* (April 22, 1837), XIV, 343. Thomas Moore had his own version of Europeanized Indians, and his "The Lake of the Dismal Swamp" may have had some effect on Chivers: But oft, from the Indian hunters' camp / This lover and maiden so true / Are seen at the hour of midnight damp / To cross the Lake by a fire-fly lamp, / And paddle their white canoe! *The Poetical Works of Thomas Moore* (Boston, 1871), II, 39.

32. *Works of Jonathan Edwards, Apocalyptic Writings* ed. Stephen J. Stein (New York, 1977), V, 99, 102, 124, 301, 97.

33. Marguerite Beck Block, *The New Church in the New World* (New York, 1932), pp. 73-78, 95-96.

34. Samuel Woodworth, *Melodies, Songs and Ballads* (New York, 1831), pp. 182-23.

35. *New Church in the New World*, pp. 95-96.

36. *Ibid.*, pp. 133-37.

37. *Correspondence of Chivers*, pp. 226-31.

38. *Emerson's Complete Works*, (Cambridge, 1883), *Swedenborg, or the Mystic*, IV, 96, 113. Since all subsequent quotations are from the same edition of Emerson only the titles of a particular work and the volume and page numbers will be given.

39. *The Over-Soul*, II, 264.

40. *The Poet*, III, 10.

41. *Language*, I, 31, 32.

42. *Ibid.*, I, 34-36.

43. *Prospects*, I, 77.

44. "Solution," IX, 191.

45. *The Centennial Edition of the Works of Sidney Lanier;* ed. Charles R. Anderson (Baltimore, 1945); *Introduction* by Anderson, I, XV. The same procedure indicated in footnote 38 will be observed.

46. *Introduction*, I, XV.

47. "Sunrise," I, 149.

48. "The Symphony," I, 49.

Chapter Three

1. *Nacoochee; or, the Beautiful Star, With Other Poems* (New York, 1837) p. v.

2. *Ibid.*, pp. v-vi. See also footnote 5 of Chapter 5 for references to Swedenborg's ideas and teachings.

3. *Ibid.*, pp. vi-vii.
4. "Nacoochee," p. 1.
5. *Ibid.*, p. 3.
6. *Ibid.*, p. 12.
7. *Ibid.*, p. 19.
8. *Ibid.*, p. 18.
9. *Ibid.*, p. 25.
10. *Ibid.*, p. 26.
11. See footnote 28 of Chapter 10.
12. "The Death of Time," p. 32.
13. See footnote 28 of Chapter Seven.
14. "The Death of Time," p. 33.
15. "The Soaring Swan," p. 36.
16. *Ibid.*, p. 38.
17. Damon, *Thomas Holley Chivers*, p. 104.
18. "Holy Love," p. 43.
19. "Man's Life," p. 61.
20. "Georgia Waters," p. 75.
21. See my book *French Romanticism on the Frontier* for a discussion of Chateaubriand's popularity in the North and South.
22. "Ode to the Mississippi," p. 92.
23. "To My Mother—Written Beyond the Mountains," p. 98.
24. "To My Sister," p. 101.
25. "Stanzas for Music," p. 106.

Chapter Four

1. Quoted in Damon, *Thomas Holley Chivers*, p. 141.
2. *Ibid.*, p. 149.
3. *The Lost Pleiad; and Other Poems* (New York, 1845), p. 3.
4. *Ibid.*, p. 8.
5. *Ibid.*, p. 6.
6. *Ibid.*, p. 12.
7. *Ibid.*, p. 14.
8. *Ibid.*, p. 15.
9. *Ibid.*, p. 16.
10. *Ibid.*, *p. 16.*
11. *See footnote 5 of Chapter 5.*
12. *Watts, Thomas Holley Chivers*, pp. 125-32.
13. *The Lost Pleiad*, p. 17.
14. *Ibid.*, p. 16.
15. *Ibid.*, p. 18.
16. *Ibid.*, p. 18.
17. *Ibid.*, p. 19.
18. *Ibid.*, p. 20.

19. *Ibid.*, p. 21.
20. See footnotes 5 and 9 of Chapter 5.
21. *The Lost Pleiad*, p. 21.
22. *Ibid.*, p. 23.
23. *Ibid.*, p. 23.
24. See my book *French Romanticism on the Frontier.*
25. *The Lost Pleiad*, p. 24.
26. *Ibid.*, p. 26.
27. *Ibid.*, p. 26.
28. *Ibid.*, p. 28.
29. *Ibid.*, p. 29.
30. *Ibid.*, p. 32.
31. *Correspondence of Thomas Holley Chivers*, p. 43.
32. It is interesting to note that Chivers himself assumed the pseudonym of Politian. See "Via Coeli, or the Way to Heaven," *Univercoelum,* III (December 9, 1848), III, 22.
33. *Search After Truth; or, A New Revelation of the Psycho-Physiological Nature of Man* (New York, 1848), p. 37.
34. *The Works of Jacob Behmen, The Teutonic Philosopher*, trans. Rev. William Law (London, 1764), I, 114; III, 488.
35. Readers wishing to undertake a more detailed study of Swedenborgian references in Chivers should consult *The Swedenborg Concordance, A Complete Work of Reference to the Theological Writings of Emanuel Swedenborg.* Ed. Rev. John Faulkner Potts, B. A. (London, 1888), 4 volumes. Other useful references are: Cyriel Odhner Sigstedt, *The Swedenborg Epic. The Life and Works of Emanuel Swedenborg* (New York, 1952); Signe Toksvig, *Emanuel Swedenborg. Scientist and Mystic* (New Haven, 1948).
36. Quoted in Frederick Hiebel, *Novalis* (Chapel Hill, 1954), p. 38.
37. *The Complete Writings of William Blake*, ed. Geoffrey Keynes (New York, 1957). "The Marriage of Heaven and Hell", p. 152.
38. Louis Claude de Saint Martin, *Tableau Naturel* (Edinburgh, 1782), II, 127.
39. *The Works of Jacob Behmen*, I, 114; III, 488.

Chapter Five

1. Chivers, "Eonchs of Ruby" *Georgia Citizen* (June 25, 1851).
2. See footnote 5 of Chapter 5.
3. *Eonchs of Ruby: A Gift of Love* (New York, 1851), p. 5.
4. *Ibid.*, p. 14.
5. *Ibid.*, p. 8.
6. *Ibid.*, p. 17.
7. *Ibid.*, p. 30.
8. *Ibid.*, p. 31.

9. *Ibid.*, p. 37.
10. *Ibid.*, p. 43.
11. *Ibid.*, p. 50.
12. *Ibid.*, p. 55.
13. *Ibid.*, p. 57.
14. Damon, *Thomas Holley Chivers*, p. 192.
15. *Eonchs of Ruby*, pp. 58-59.
16. Damon, *Thomas Holley Chivers*, pp. 192-93.
17. Watts, *Thomas Holley Chivers*, pp. 163-64.
18. *Eonchs of Ruby*, p. 66.
19. *Ibid.*, p. 82.
20. *Ibid.*, p. 82. Baudelaire explains his poem on one of Delacroix's paintings in *Curiosités esthétiques* (Paris, 1868).
21. *Ibid.*, p. 83.
22. *Ibid.*, pp. 86-87.
23. *Ibid.*, p. 92.
24. *Ibid.*, p. 96.
25. *Ibid.*, p. 98.
26. *Ibid.*, p. 102.
27. *Ibid.*, p. 106.
28. *Ibid.*, p. 106.
29. *Ibid.*, p. 109.
30. *Ibid.*, p. 117.
31. *Ibid.*, pp. 120-21.
32. *Ibid.*, p. 130.
33. *Ibid.*, p. 136.
34. *Ibid.*, pp. 142-43.
35. *Ibid.*, p. 145.
36. *Ibid.*, p. 153.
37. *Ibid.*, p. 157.
38. *Ibid.*, p. 160.
39. *Ibid.*, p. 165.

Chapter Six

1. *Atlanta: or the True Blessed Island of Poesy: A Paul Epic in Three Lustra* (Macon, Georgia, 1853) p. 3.
2. *Ibid.*, p. 3.
3. *Ibid.*, p. 4.
4. *Ibid.*, p. 5.
5. *Ibid.*, p. 5.
6. Damon, *Thomas Holley Chivers*, p. 243.
7. *Atlanta*, p. 3.
8. *Selected Writings of Edgar Allan Poe*, ed. Edward H. Davidson (Cambridge, Mass., 1956), "The Poetic Principle," p. 464.

9. *Atlanta*, p. 5.
10. "The Poetic Principle", p. 464.
11. *Atlanta*, p. 5.
12. "The Poetic Principle", p. 469.
13. *Atlanta*, p. 3.
14. *Ibid.*, p. 7.
15. *Ibid.*, p. 9.
16. *Ibid.*, p. 14.
17. *Ibid.*, pp. 21-22.
18. *Ibid.*, p. 23.
19. *Ibid.*, p. 24.
20. *Ibid.*, p. 24.
21. *Ibid.*, p. 3.

Chapter Seven

1. *Memoralia; or, Phials of Amber Full of the Tears of Love* (Philadelphia, 1853), p. vii.
2. *Ibid.*, p. ix.
3. *Ibid.*, p. ix.
4. *Ibid.*, pp. ix-x.
5. *Ibid.*, p. xii.
6. *Ibid.*, p. xiii.
7. See footnote 5 of Chapter Five.
8. *Memoralia*, p. 15.
9. *Ibid.*, p. 24.

Chapter Eight

1. *Virginalia; or, Songs of My Summer Nights* (Philadelphia, 1853), pp. iii-iv.
2. See footnote 5 of Chapter Five.
3. *Virginalia*, p. v.
4. *Ibid.*, p. 12.
5. *Ibid.*, p. 19.
6. Bayard Taylor, *The Echo Club and Other Literary Diversions* (Boston, 1876), pp. 53-54.
7. *Virginalia*, p. 24.
8. *Ibid.*, p. 26.
9. *Ibid.*, p. 26.
10. *Ibid.*, p. 30.
11. *Ibid.*, p. 32.
12. *Ibid.*, p. 75.
13. *Ibid.*, p. 85.
14. *Ibid.*, p. 45.

15. *Ibid.*, p. 42.

16. Theophilus O'Flanagan, "Observations on the Gaelic Language," *Transactions of the Gaelic Society of Dublin*, (Dublin, 1808), I, vii.

17. Moore, *Irish Melodies* (Philadelphia, 1815), pp. 92-93.

Chapter Nine

1. *Correspondence of Thomas Holley Chivers*, pp, 8, 13.

2. Richard Beale Davis, ed. *Chivers' Life of Poe* (New York, 1952), pp. 9-21.

3. Unless otherwise stated, the material and information in this chapter are taken from Davis, *Chivers' Life of Poe*.

4. John Forster, "American Poets," *Foreign Quarterly Review* (January, 1844), XXXII, 318-19.

5. Poe, *The Literati* (New York, 1850), p. 570.

6. Watts, *Thomas Holley Chivers*, pp. 152-56.

7. "The Valley of Diamonds," *Georgia Citizen* (July 12, 1850).

8. "Eonchs of Ruby," *Georgia Citizen* (June 8, 1851).

9. "Origin of Poe's Raven," *Waverly Magazine* (July 30, 1852), p. 73.

10. *The Correspondence of Thomas Holley Chivers*, p. 138.

11. *Ibid.*, p. 107.

12. *Ibid.*, p. 114.

13. See following articles in *Waverly Magazine* (August 13, 1853), p. 105; H. S. Cornwell, "A Croak from the 'Raven' " and J. J. P., "Edgar A. Poe."

14. *The Correspondence of Thomas Holley Chivers*, p. 210.

15. From a manuscript in the Chivers collection in Duke University Library.

16. *The Correspondence of Thomas Holley Chivers*, p. 70.

17. *The Lost Pleiad*, p. 26.

18. Damon, *Thomas Holley Chivers*, pp. 214-16.

19. See Damon and Watts.

20. "Origin of Poe's Raven," *Georgia Citizen* (September 22, 1854).

Chapter Ten

1. A. B. Longstreet, *Georgia Scenes, Characters, Incidents, etc., In the First Half Century of the Republic, By a Native Georgian* (New York, 1840), p. 15.

2. *Ibid.*, p. 45.

3. George Pullen Jackson, *White and Negro Spirituals* (New York: Augustin, 1943), pp. 121-25.

4. William Walker, *The Southern Harmony Songbook*, reproduced with an introduction by the Federal Writer's Project of Kentucky, Works Progress Administration (New York, 1939), p. 313.

5. *Ibid.*, pp. 99.

6. *Ibid.*, p. xxix.

7. See Allen D. Carden, *The Missouri Harmony* (Cincinnati, 1837), William Houser; *The Hesperian Harp; A Collection of Psalm and Hymn Tunes* (Philadelphia, 1848); W. H. Swan, *The Harp of Columbia; A New System of Sacred Music* (Knoxville, Tenn., 1848).

8. *Harp of Columbia*, p. 184.

9. *The Path of Sorrow*, p. 25. Reference is made to various folk instruments in "On the Death of Adaline."

10. "Letters from the North," *Georgia Citizen* (May 3, 1851).

11. "Death of the Devil, A Serio-Ludrico, Tragico-Comico, Nigero-Whitemano Extravaganza," *Georgia Citizen* (November 13, 1852).

12. "Death of the Devil," *Georgia Citizen* (November 20, 1852).

13. "Death of the Devil," *Georgia Citizen* (December 4, 1852).

14. *Ibid.*, (December 4, 1852).

15. "The Silent Voice" from the Chivers' manuscript collection at Duke University Library.

16. *Correspondence of Thomas Holley Chivers*, p. 259.

17. Ralph B. Flanders, *Plantation Slavery in Georgia* (Chapel Hill, 1933), pp. 266-86.

18. *Ibid.*, pp. 152-53.

19. Dorothy Scarborough, *On the Trail of Negro Folk Songs* (Cambridge, 1925), pp. 206-10.

20. John A. Lomax and Alan Lomax, *Negro Folk Songs as Sung by Lead Belly* (New York, 1936), pp. ix-xiv.

21. Scarborough, *On the Trail of Negro Folk Songs*, pp. 238-40.

22. Alan Lomax, *The Folk Songs of North America*, (London, 1960), pp. 448-52.

23. "Letters from New York," *Georgia Citizen* (March 1, 1851).

24. *Ibid.*, (March 1, 1851).

25. "Letters from the North," *Georgia Citizen* (May 3, 1851).

26. *Ibid.*, (July 3, 1852).

27. "Corn-Shucking Song," *Georgia Citizen* (June 23, 1855).

28. George E. Woodberry, "The Poe-Chivers Papers," *The Century Magazine* (February, 1903), p. 555.

29. *Ibid.*, p. 555.

30. From Chivers' collection in Duke University Library.

31. Chivers, "The Editor's Table," *The Knickerbocker, or New York Magazine* (August, 1851), p. 181.

32. *Ibid.*, p. 181.

33. From manuscript collection in Duke University Library.

34. Jay B. Hubbell, *The South in American Literature* 1607-1900 (Durham, N.C., 1954), pp. 554-55.

35. Woodberry, "The Poe-Chivers Papers," p. 555.

36. *Virginalia*, p. 24.

37. *Eonchs of Ruby*, pp. 49-50.

144   THOMAS HOLLEY CHIVERS

38. *Nacoochee,* pp. 49-50.
39. "The Roll of Fame," *Spiritual Telegraph,* III (September 9, 1854), 75.
40. *Nacoochee,* pp. 36-37.
41. *Eonchs of Ruby,* pp. 57-58.
42. *Virginalia,* p. 108.
43. "The Little Boy Blue," *Waverly Magazine* VII (July 30, 1853), 71.
44. "Chinese Serenade," *Dodge Literary Museum,* V (October 30, 1852), 344.
45. *Ibid.,* p. 344.
46. "Railroad Song," *Georgia Citizen* (June 21, 1851).
47. "Caelicola," *Peterson's Magazine,* XVII (February, 1850), 102.
48. *Paths of Sorrow,* p. 116.
49. *Nacoochee,* pp. 61-62.
50. *Eonchs of Ruby,* p. 157.
51. *Virginalia,* p. 113.

Chapter Fourteen

1. "Presumption Rebuked," *Georgia Citizen* (May 17, 1850).
2. "The Great Know Nothing," *Georgia Citizen* (April 7, 1854).
3. "Professor Longfellow's Hiawatha," *Georgia Citizen* (January 9, 1856).
4. "Letters from the North," *Georgia Citizen* (July 14, 1851).
5. See my article "An Old New York Salon-French Style," *New York Historical Society Quarterly,* LV (January, 1971), 38-51.
6. "Eonchs of Ruby," *Georgia Citizen* (June 28, 1851).
7. "The Valley of Diamonds," *Georgia Citizen* (February 22, 1851).
8. *Correspondence of Thomas Holley Chivers,* pp. 150-51.
9. W. C. Richards, "Bibliographical Record," *The Orion,* II (March-April, 1843), 370-72.
10. Augustine Duganne, *Parnassus in Pillory* (New York, 1851), p. 81.
11. Augustine Duganne, "Eonchs of Ruby," *The Message Bird* (December 16, 1850), pp. 561-62.
12. Watts, *Thomas Holley Chivers,* p. 37.
13. Bayard Taylor, *The Echo Club and other Diversions* (Boston, 1876).
14. Charles A. Dana, "Literary Chat," *The Times* (Chattanooga, Tenn.), (March 5, 1899).
15. James A. Harrison, "Poe and Chivers," *The Complete Works of Edgar Allan Poe* (New York 1902), VII, 266-88.
16. Thomas Olive Mabbott, "Kilmer and Chivers," *The New York Times* (June 4, 1933).
17. Damon, *Thomas Holley Chivers,* pp. xiv. 237.
18. "The Chinese Serenade for the Ut-Kam and Tong-Koo," *Dodge's Literary Museum,* V (October 30, 1852), 344. The poem beginning with a two syllable line and then increasing in number to indicate the rising crescendo recalls in its structure a technique used by Victor Hugo in "*Les Djinns,*" a

poem very popular and widely translated in American journals of Chivers'
day.

19. "The Railroad Song," *Georgia Citizen* (June 21, 1851).

20. Landon C. Bell, *Poe and Chivers* (Columbus, Ohio: 1931).

21. See Watts and Damon, *Thomas Holley Chivers.*

22. Jay B. Hubbell, *The South in American Literature* (Durham, 1954),
pp. 555-59.

23. Edmund Clarence Stedman, *Poets of America* (Boston and New York,
1885), p. 250.

24. Damon, *Thomas Holley Chivers,* pp. 272-73.

25. W. M. Rossetti, *Rossetti Papers, 1862 to 1870* (New York, 1930), pp.
180-81.

26. Damon, *Thomas Holley Chivers,* pp. 272-73.

27. *Ibid.,* pp. 272-73.

28. *Correspondence of Thomas Holley Chivers,* pp. 186-87.

29. See C. M. Bowra, *The Heritage of Symbolism* (London, 1943); Joseph
Chiari, *Symbolism from Poe to Mallarmé* (London, 1956); Edmund Wilson,
Axel's Castle (New York, 1931).

Selected Bibliography

Chivers' Works in Chronological Order

1. Books

The Path of Sorrow, or, The Lament of Youth: A Poem. Franklin, Tenn.: *Western Weekly Review*, 1832.

Conrad and Eudora; or, The Death of Alonzo. A Tragedy. In Five Acts. Founded on the Murder of Sharpe, by Beauchamp, in Kentucky. Philadelphia: 1834.

Nacoochee; or, The Beautiful Star, with Other Poems. New York: W. E. Dean, 1837.

The Lost Pleiad; and Other Poems. New York: Edward O. Jenkins, 1845.

Eonchs of Ruby, A Gift of Love. New York: Spalding and Shephard, 1851.

Memoralia; or, Phials of Amber Full of the Tears of Love. A Gift for the Beautiful. Philadelphia: Lippincott, 1853.

Virginalia; or, Songs of My Summer Nights. A Gift of Love for the Beautiful. Philadelphia: Lippincott, 1853.

The Sons of Usna: A Tragi-Apotheosis, in Five Acts. Philadelphia: C. Sherman, 1858.

Chivers' Life of Poe. Ed. Richard Beale Davis. New York: Dutton, 1952.

The Correspondence of Thomas Holly Chivers. Ed. Emma Lester Chase and Lois Ferry Parks. Providence, Rhode Island: Brown University Press, 1957. This work was originally intended as the first volume of a complete set of Chivers' works.

2. Works in Manuscript.

A considerable body of unpublished material by Chivers in the form of plays, stories, and criticism is available in the Duke University Library.

3. Pamphlets.

The Constitution of Man. Memphis, Tenn.: 1833. (Title from the *Western Monthly Magazine*, July 1833, I, 321-25).

Search After Truth; or, A New Revelation of the Psycho-Physiological Nature of Man. New York: Cobb & Yallalee, 1848.

Atlanta: or, The True Blessed Island of Poesy, A Paul Epic–In Three Lustra. Macon, Georgia: *Georgia Citizen*, 1853.

146

Birth-Day Song of Liberty. A Paean of Glory for the Heroes of Freedom. Atlanta, Georgia: C. R. Hanleiter, 1856.

4. Works published in magazines.
  Chivers published his poems in over seventy different magazines. In many cases, the same poem was reprinted in another journal. As yet, there is no definitive bibliography of his works published in magazines.

5. Works published in reprint editions.
  Conrad and Eudora; Birthday-Song Liberty. Ed. Charles M. Lombard. Delmar, New York: Scholars' Facsimiles and Reprints, 1978. *Nacoochee.* Ed. Charles M. Lombard. Delmar, New York: Scholars' Facsimiles and Reprints, 1977. *Search After Truth; The Lost Pleiad; Atlanta.* Ed. Charles M. Lombard; Delmar, New York: Scholars Facsimiles and Reprints, 1976. *Virginalia.* Ed. E.L. Schwab. Brooklyn, Research Classics, 1942.

SECONDARY SOURCES

1. Bibliography
S. Foster Damon's *Thomas Holley Chivers* has a useful list of some of the poems and articles the Georgian published in current magazines. There are also reviews and criticisms of his works that appeared during his lifetime.

2. Principal works on Chivers.
DAMON, S. FOSTER. *Thomas Holley Chivers, Friend of Poe.* New York: Harpers, 1930. This scholarly and comprehensive study is a must for the researcher.
BELL, LANDON C. *Poe and Chivers.* Columbus: Trowbridge, 1931. A biased attack on Damon's praise of Chivers', useful only as a reflection of the persistence of misconceptions of the Georgian.
BENTON, JOEL. *In the Poe Circle.* New York: Mansfield &Wessels, 1899. A fair and concise summary of the Poe-Chivers controversy and of the relationship between the two poets.
HARRISON, JAMES A. "Poe and Chivers." *The Complete Works of Edgar Allan Poe.* VII, 266-88. New York: T. Y. Crowell, 1902. Harrison's comments are useful if the reader is aware of the limited state of research on Chivers in 1902 that hampered Harrison's judgment.
WATTS, CHARLES HENRY. *Thomas Holley Chivers, His Literary Career and Poetry.* Athens, Georgia: University of Georgia Press, 1956. Watts' book, along with Damon's work, is an indispensable starting point for a study of Chivers. One work complements the other.

Index